The GUITAR STRUMMERS'
Christmas Songbook

PREFACE

This book is designed especially to get you playing (and singing!) along with your favorite Christmas songs. The songs are arranged in lead sheet format, giving you the chords, melody, and lyrics. Strum patterns are also written above the staff as an accompaniment suggestion. Strum the chords in the rhythm indicated. Use the chord diagrams found at the top of the first page of the arrangement for the appropriate chord voicings.

ISBN 0-634-04864-3

HAL•LEONARD®
CORPORATION
7777 W. BLUEMOUND RD. P.O. BOX 13819 MILWAUKEE, WI 53213

Visit Hal Leonard Online at
www.halleonard.com

The GUITAR STRUMMERS' Christmas Songbook

CONTENTS

All Through the Night

Welsh Folksong

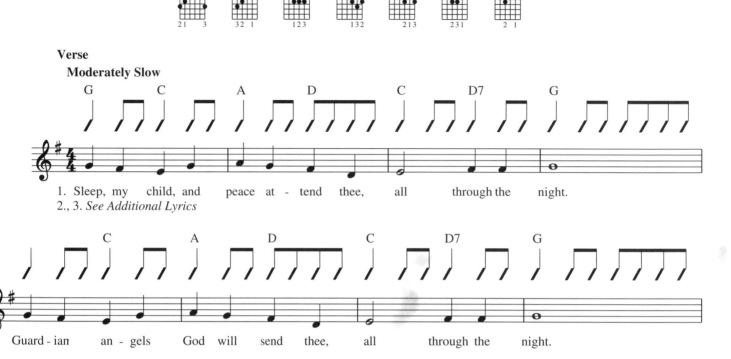

Verse

Moderately Slow

1. Sleep, my child, and peace at-tend thee, all through the night.
2., 3. *See Additional Lyrics*

Guard-ian an-gels God will send thee, all through the night.

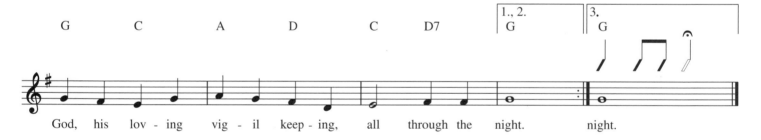

cont. rhy. sim.

Soft, the drow-sy hours are creep-ing, hill and vale in slum-ber sleep-ing.

God, his lov-ing vig-il keep-ing, all through the night. night.

Additional Lyrics

2. While the moon, her watch is keeping,
   All through the night.
   While the weary world is sleeping,
   All through the night.
   Through your dreams you're swiftly stealing,
   Visions of delight revealing,
   Christmas time is so appealing,
   All through the night.

3. You, my God, a babe of wonder,
   All through the night.
   Dreams you can't break from thunder,
   All Through the night.
   Children's dreams cannot be broken,
   Life is but a lovely token.
   Christmas should be softly spoken,
   All through the night.

Almost Day

Words and Music by Huddie Ledbetter

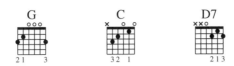

Verse
Moderate Square Dance

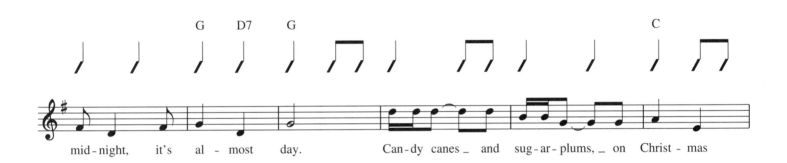

1. Chick-ens a-crowin' for mid-night, _ it's al-most day. Chick-ens a-crowin' for
2. *See Additional Lyrics*

mid-night, it's al-most day. Can-dy canes _ and sug-ar-plums, _ on Christ-mas

Day. Can-dy canes _ and sug-ar-plums, _ on Christ-mas Day. Day.

Additional Lyrics

2. Mama'll stuff a turkey on Christmas Day.
   Mama'll stuff a turkey on Christmas Day.
   Santa Claus is coming on Christmas Day.
   Santa Claus is coming on Christmas Day.

Angels We Have Heard on High

Traditional French Carol
Translated by James Chadwick

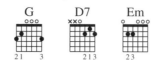

Additional Lyrics

2. Shepherds why this jubilee,
   Why your joyous strains prolong?
   What the gladsome tidings be
   Which inspire your heavenly song?

Ave Maria

By Franz Schubert

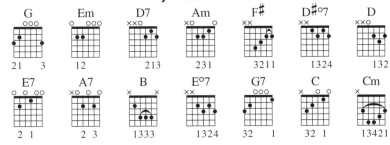

Verse

Reverently

1. A — ve Ma - ri - a! Gra - ti - a — ple - na, Ma-
2. *See additional lyrics*

ri - a — gra - ti - a ple - na, Ma - ri - a gra - ti - a — ple - na, A -

ve, _____ A - ve! Do - mi - nus, _____ Do - mi - nus — te - cum, Be - ne -

dic - ta tu in mu - li - e - re - bus et be - ne - dic - - - tus, et

be - ne - dic - tus, fruc - tus ven - tris, ven - tris tu - i, Je - - - sus.

A - ve Ma - ri - a!

Additional Lyrics

2. Ave Maria!
   Mater Dei, Ora pro nobis peccatoribus,
   Ora ora pro nobis, Ora, ra pro nobis peccatoribus.
   None et in hora mortis, in hora mortis nostrae,
   In hora mortis, mortis nostrae,
   In hora mortis nostrae.
   Ave Maria!

Away in a Manger

Anonymous Text (vv. 1, 2)
Text by John T. McFarland (v. 3)
Music by Jonathan E. Spillman

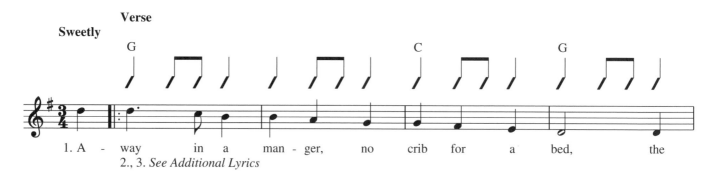

Verse

Sweetly

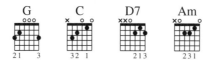

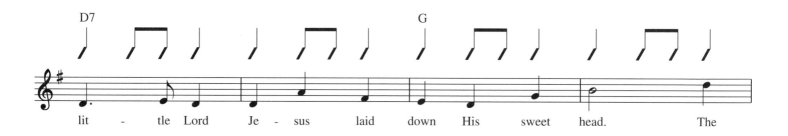

1. A - way in a man - ger, no crib for a bed, the
2., 3. *See Additional Lyrics*

lit - tle Lord Je - sus laid down His sweet head. The

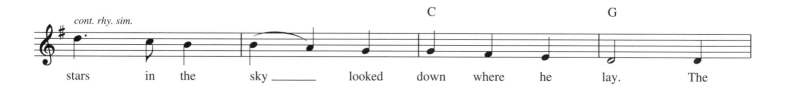

stars in the sky _____ looked down where he lay. The

lit - tle Lord Je - sus a - sleep on the hay. 2. The there.

Additional Lyrics

2. The cattle are lowing, the baby awakes,
   But little Lord Jesus, no crying He makes.
   I love Thee, Lord Jesus, look down from the sky
   And stay by my cradle 'til morning is nigh.

3. Be near me, Lord Jesus, I ask Thee to stay
   Close by me forever and love me I pray.
   Bless all the dear children in Thy tender care
   And take us to heaven to live with Thee there.

Bring a Torch, Jeannette, Isabella

17th Century French Provencal Carol

Additional Lyrics

2. Hasten now, good folk of the village,
Hasten now, the Christ Child to see.
You will find him asleep in a manger,
Quietly come and whisper softly.
Hush, hush, peacefully how He slumbers,
Hush, hush, peacefully how He sleeps.

Because It's Christmas
(For All the Children)

Music by Barry Manilow
Lyric by Bruce Sussman and Jack Feldman

Verse
Moderately Slow

1. To-night the stars __ shine __ for the chil - dren and light the way for dreams to
2. *See Additional Lyrics*

fly.

To-night our love comes wrapped in _____ rib - bons.

The world is right and hopes are high. And from a dark __ and frost - ed

win - dow a child __ ap - pears to search __ the sky be - cause __ it's

1. Christ-mas, be-cause it's Christ-mas.

2. Christ-mas for now __ and for-ev - er for all __ of the

Additional Lyrics

2. Tonight belongs to all the children.
   Tonight their joy rings through the air.
   And so, we send our tender blessings
   To all the children ev'rywhere
   To see the smiles and hear the laughter,
   A time to give, a time to share
   Because it's Christmas for now and forever
   For all of the children in us all.

C-H-R-I-S-T-M-A-S

Words by Jenny Lou Carson
Music by Eddy Arnold

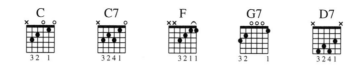

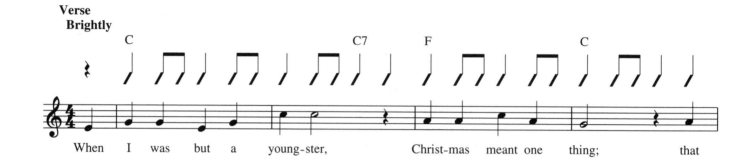

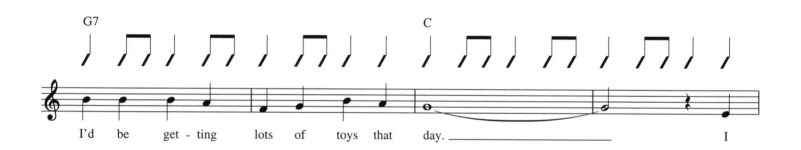

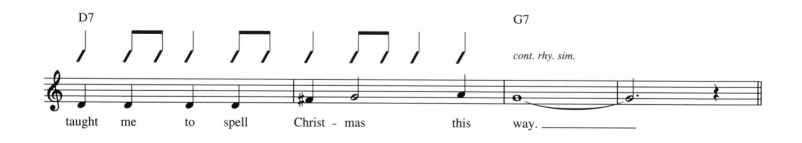

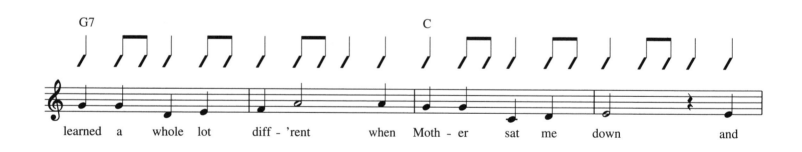

Verse
Brightly

When I was but a young-ster, Christ-mas meant one thing; that I'd be get-ting lots of toys that day. _____ I learned a whole lot diff-'rent when Moth-er sat me down and taught me to spell Christ-mas this way. _____

cont. rhy. sim.

Chorus

"C" is for the Christ child born up - on this day,

"H" for her - ald an - gels in the night. _____

"R" means our Re - deem - er, "I" means Is - ra - el.

"S" is for the star that shone so bright. _____

"T" is for three wise men, they who trav - eled far.

"M" is for the man - ger where He lay. _____

"A"'s for all He stands for, "S" means shep - herds came and

that's why there's a Christ - mas day. _____

The Christmas Song
(Chestnuts Roasting on an Open Fire)

Music and Lyric by Mel Torme and Robert Wells

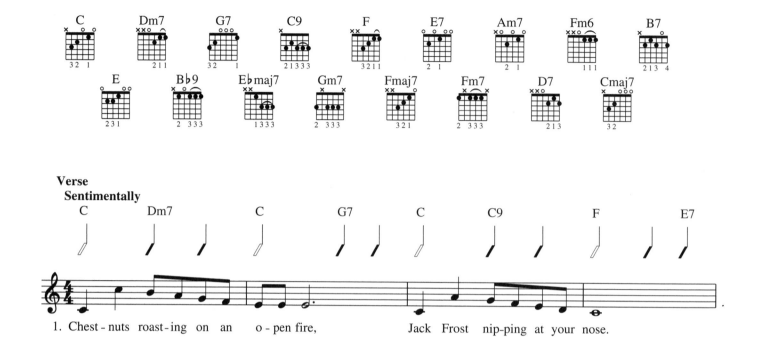

Verse
Sentimentally

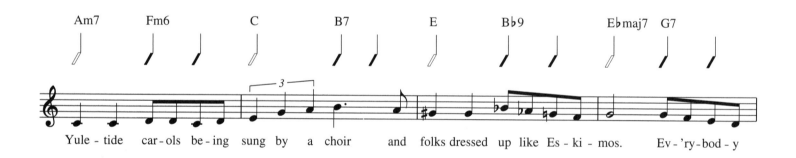

1. Chest - nuts roast - ing on an o - pen fire, Jack Frost nip - ping at your nose.

Yule - tide car - ols be - ing sung by a choir and folks dressed up like Es - ki - mos. Ev - 'ry - bod - y

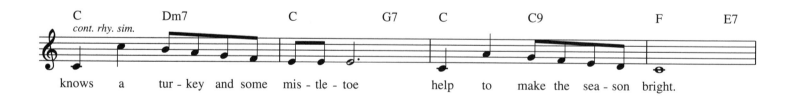

knows a tur - key and some mis - tle - toe help to make the sea - son bright.

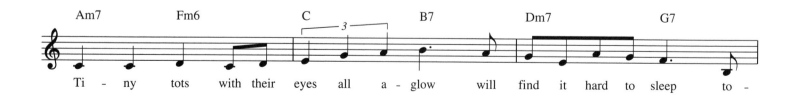

Ti - ny tots with their eyes all a - glow will find it hard to sleep to -

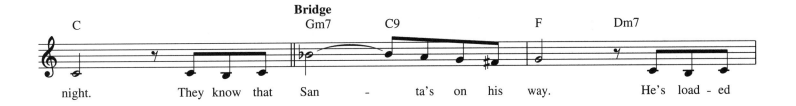

Bridge

night. They know that San - ta's on his way. He's load - ed

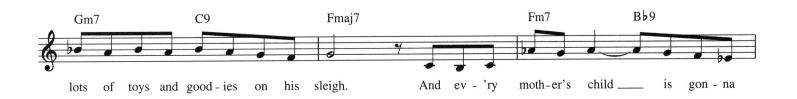

lots of toys and good - ies on his sleigh. And ev - 'ry moth - er's child ____ is gon - na

spy ____ to see if rein - deer ____ real - ly know how to fly. 2. And

Verse

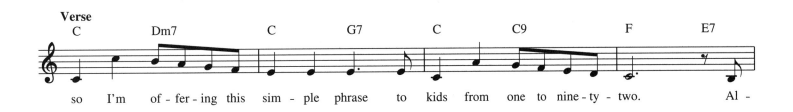

so I'm of - fer - ing this sim - ple phrase to kids from one to nine - ty - two. Al -

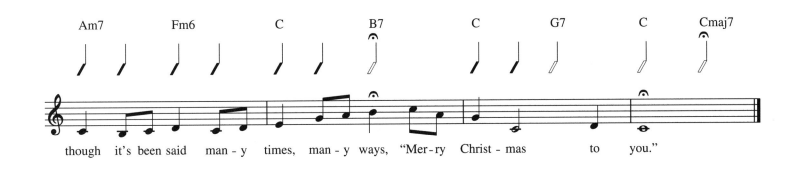

though it's been said man - y times, man - y ways, "Mer - ry Christ - mas to you."

Christmas Time Is Here

from A CHARLIE BROWN CHRISTMAS

Words by Lee Mendelson
Music by Vince Guaraldi

Coventry Carol

Words by Robert Croo
Traditional English Melody

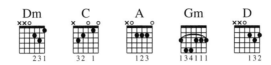

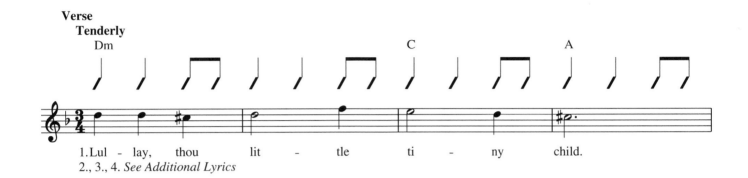

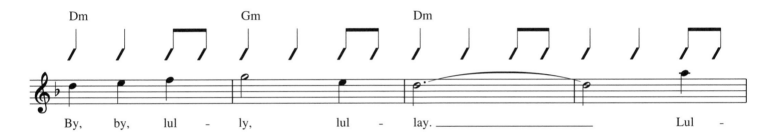

Additional Lyrics

2. Oh, sisters too,
   How may we do,
   For to preserve this day?
   This poor youngling,
   For whom we sing
   By, by, lully lullay.

3. Herod the king,
   In his raging,
   Charged he hath this day.
   His men of might,
   In his own sight,
   All young children to slay.

4. That woe is me,
   Poor child for thee!
   And ever morn and day,
   For thy parting
   Neither say nor sing
   By, by, lully lullay!

Dance of the Sugar Plum Fairy

from THE NUTCRACKER

By Pyotr Il'yich Tchaikovsky

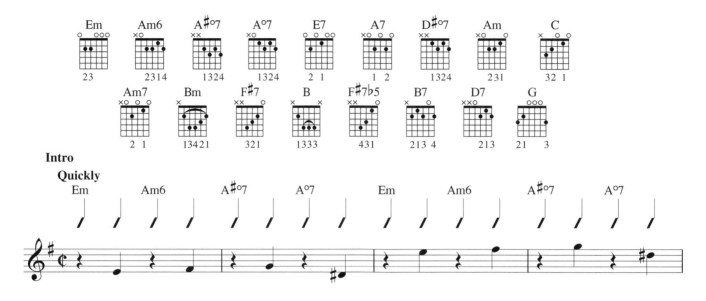

Intro

Quickly

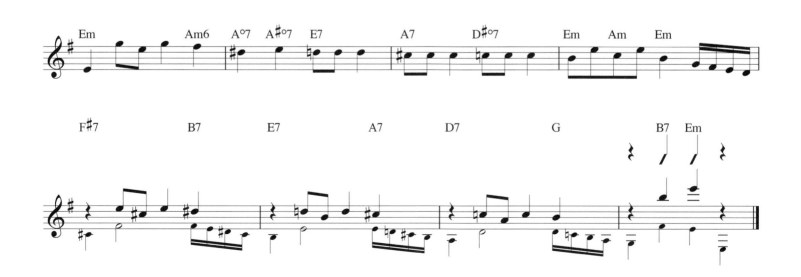

Deck the Hall

Traditional Welsh Carol

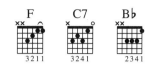

Additional Lyrics

2. See the blazing yule before us;
   Fa, la, la, la, la, la, la, la, la.
   Strike the harp and join the chorus;
   Fa, la, la, la, la, la, la, la, la.
   Follow me in merry measure;
   Fa, la, la, la, la, la, la, la, la.
   While I tell of Yuletide treasure.
   Fa, la, la, la, la, la, la, la, la.

3. Fast away the old year passes;
   Fa, la, la, la, la, la, la, la, la.
   Hail the new ye lads and lasses;
   Fa, la, la, la, la, la, la, la, la.
   Sing we joyous, all together;
   Fa, la, la, la, la, la, la, la, la.
   Heedless of the wind and weather;
   Fa, la, la, la, la, la, la, la, la.

Do They Know

Words and Music by Nathan Morris

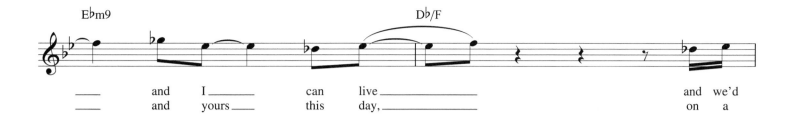

and I ___ can live _____ and we'd
and yours ___ this day, _____ on a

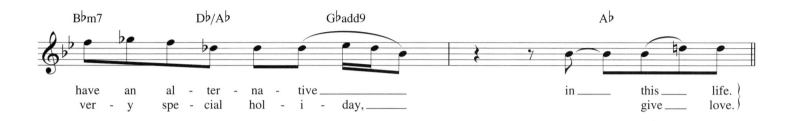

have an al - ter - na - tive _____ in ___ this ___ life. }
ver - y spe - cial hol - i - day, _____ give ___ love. }

Chorus

Do they know ___ what ___ this day means, ___ do they know

where we've been ___ and how ___ it should be? Tell me, do ___ they know? ___

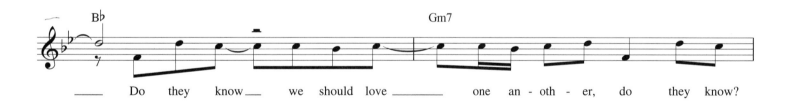

___ Do they know ___ we should love ___ one an - oth - er, do they know?

To Coda ⊕

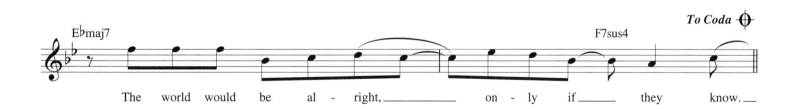

The world would be al - right, _____ on - ly if ___ they know.

Interlude

2nd time, D.C. al Coda

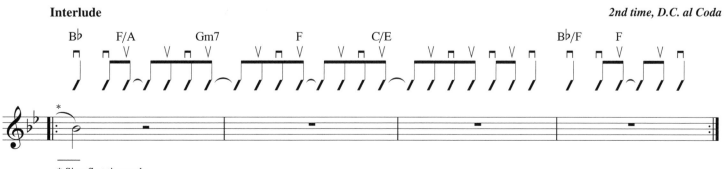

* Sing first time only

Coda

Bridge

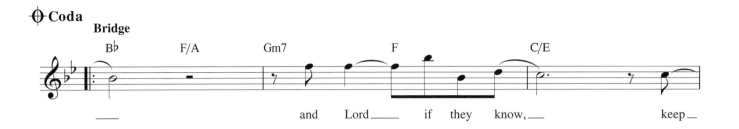

       and   Lord   if   they   know,   keep

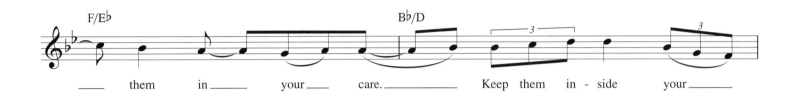

    them   in   your   care.   Keep them in - side   your

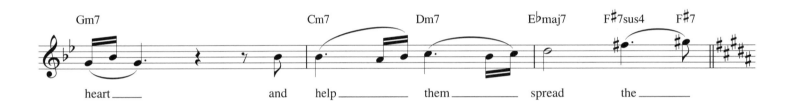

heart   and   help   them   spread   the

Outro-Chorus

word. Do   they   know   what   this   day means,   do they know

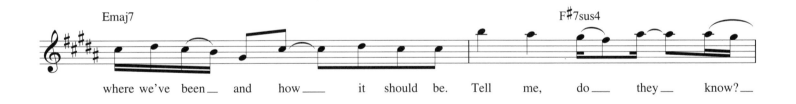

where we've been   and   how   it   should be. Tell   me,   do   they   know?

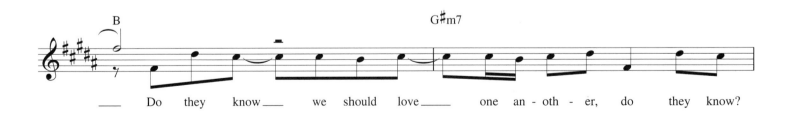

    Do   they   know   we   should   love   one an - oth - er, do   they   know?

Repeat and fade

The   world   would   be   al - right,   on - ly   if   they   know.

Do They Know It's Christmas?

Words and Music by M. Ure and B. Geldof

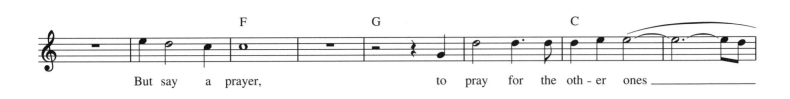

But say a prayer, to pray for the oth-er ones ____

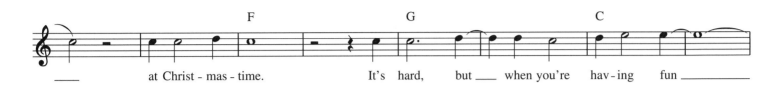

____ at Christ-mas-time. It's hard, but ____ when you're hav-ing fun ____

____ there's ____ a ____ world out - side your win - dow, ____ and it's a

world of ____ dread and fear ____ where the on - ly wa - ter

flow - ing is ____ the bit - ter sting of tears. And the

Christ-mas bells ____ that ring ____ there ____ are the clang-ing chimes of doom. ____

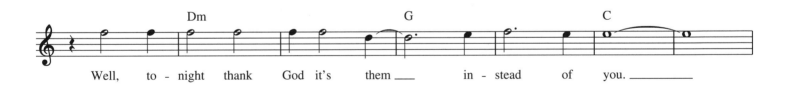

Well, to - night thank God it's them ____ in - stead of you. ____

And there won't be snow ____ in Af - ri - ca ____ this Christ -

- mas - time, ____ the great - est gift ____ they'll

Do You Hear What I Hear

Words and Music by Noel Regney and Gloria Shayne

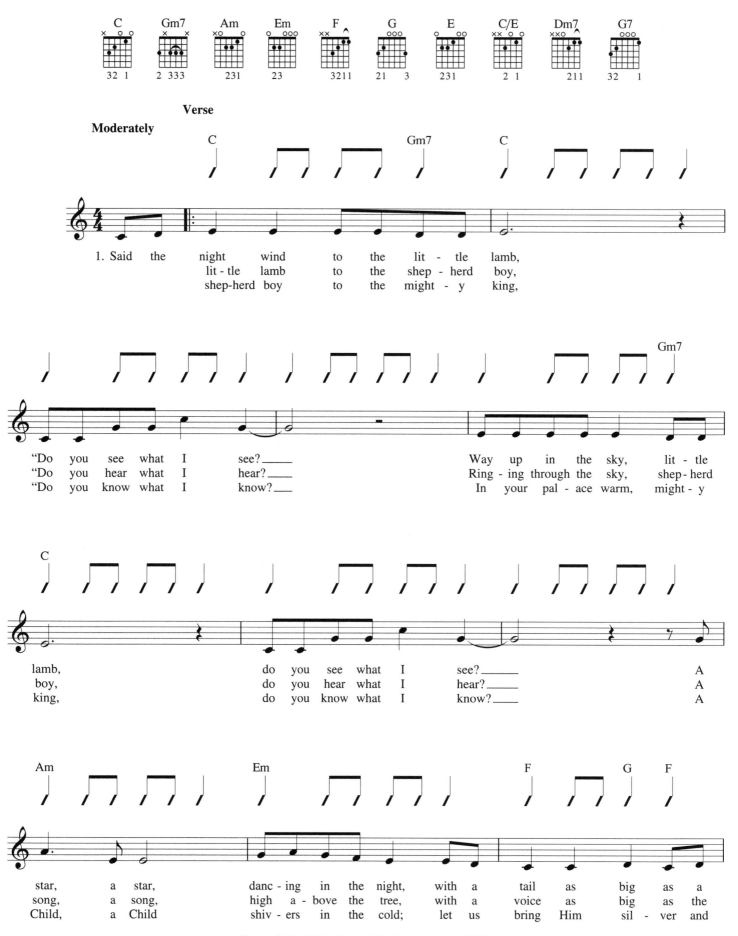

Feliz Navidad

Music and Lyrics by Jose Feliciano

Go, Tell It on the Mountain

African-American Spiritual

Verses by John W. Work, Jr.

Additional Lyrics

2. The shepherds feared and trembled
   When, lo! above the earth
   Rang out the angel chorus
   That hailed our Savior's birth.

3. Down in a lowly manger
   Our humble Christ was born.
   And God sent us salvation
   That blessed Christmas morn.

The First Noël

17th Century English Carol
Music from W. Sandys' Christmas Carols

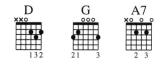

Verse
Moderately slow

1. The ___ first ___ No - ël, the ___ an - gel did
2. - 5. *See additional lyrics*

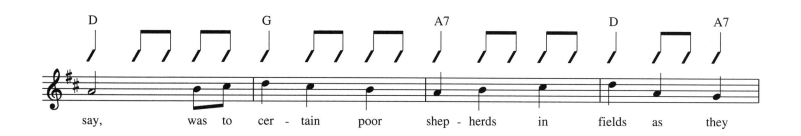

say, was to cer - tain poor shep - herds in fields as they

lay. In ___ fields ___ where ___ they lay ___ keep - ing their

sheep, on a cold win - ter's night ___ that was ___ so deep. No -

Chorus

ël, _____ No - ël, No - ël, No - ël,

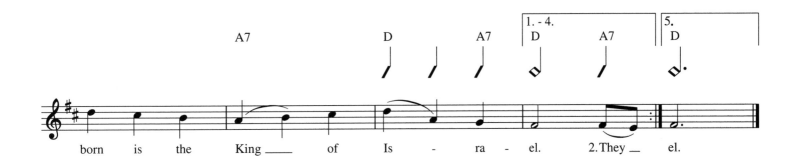

born is the King ____ of Is - ra - el. 2. They __ el.

Additional Lyrics

2. They looked up and saw a star
   Shining in the East, beyond them far.
   And to the earth it gave great light
   And so it continued both day and night.

3. And by the light of that same star,
   Three wise men came from country far;
   To seek for a King was their intent,
   And to follow the star wherever it went.

4. This star drew nigh to the northwest,
   O'er Bethlehem it took it's rest;
   And there it did both stop and stay,
   Right over the place where Jesus lay.

5. Then entered in those wise men three,
   Full reverently upon their knee;
   And offered there in His presence,
   Their gold, and myrrh, and frankincense.

Frosty the Snow Man

Words and Music by Steve Nelson and Jack Rollins

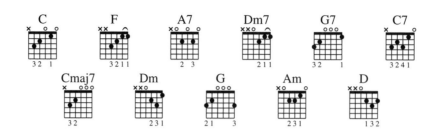

Verse
Moderately Fast

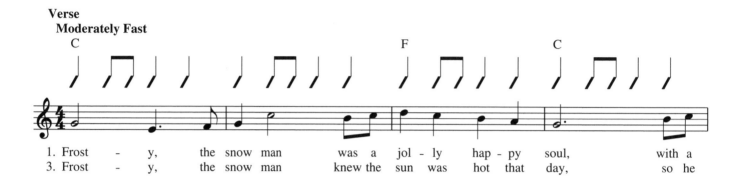

1. Frost - y, the snow man was a jol - ly hap - py soul, with a
3. Frost - y, the snow man knew the sun was hot that day, so he

corn cob pipe and a but - ton nose and two eyes made out of coal.
said, "Let's run and we'll have some fun now be - fore I melt a - way."

cont. rhy. sim.

Frost - y the snow man is a fair - y tale they say. He was
Down to the vil - lage with a broom - stick in his hand, run - ning

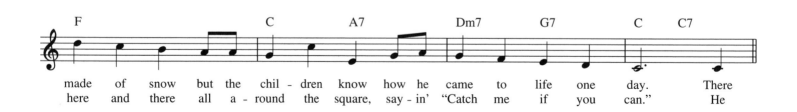

made of snow but the chil - dren know how he came to life one day. There
here and there all a - round the square, say - in' "Catch me if you can." He

Bridge

must have been some mag - ic in that old silk hat they found, for
let them down the streets of town right to the traf - fic cop, and he

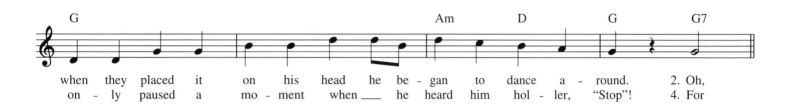

when they placed it on his head he be - gan to dance a - round. 2. Oh,
on - ly paused a mo - ment when ___ he heard him hol - ler, "Stop"! 4. For

Verse

Frost - y the snow - man was a - live as he could be, and the
Frost - y the snow man had to hur - ry on his way, but he

chil - dren say he could laugh and play just the same as you and me.
waved good - bye say - in' "Don't you cry, I'll be back a - gain some day."

Outro

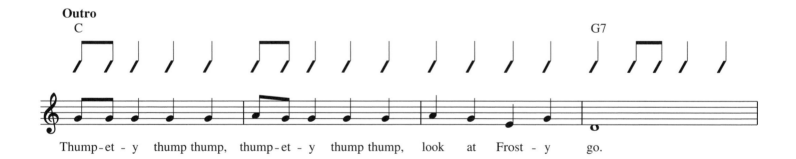

Thump - et - y thump thump, thump - et - y thump thump, look at Frost - y go.

Thump - et - y thump thump, thump - et - y thump thump, o - ver the hills of snow.

God Rest Ye Merry, Gentlemen

19th Century English Carol

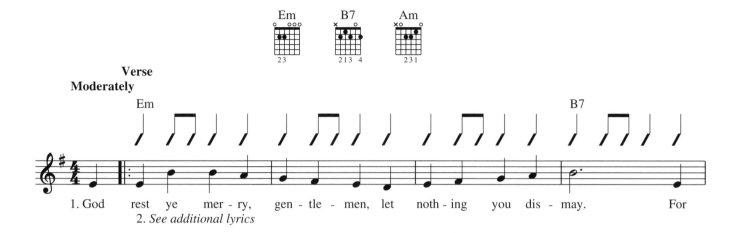

Verse
Moderately

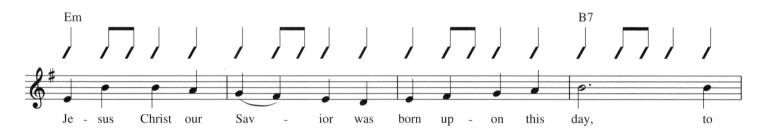

1. God rest ye mer - ry, gen - tle - men, let noth - ing you dis - may. For
2. *See additional lyrics*

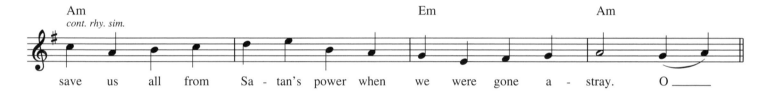

Je - sus Christ our Sav - ior was born up - on this day, to

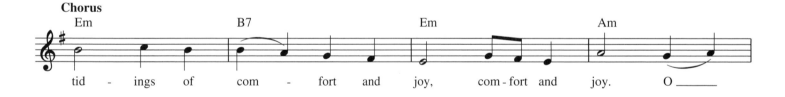

cont. rhy. sim.

save us all from Sa - tan's power when we were gone a - stray. O _____

Chorus

tid - ings of com - fort and joy, com - fort and joy. O _____

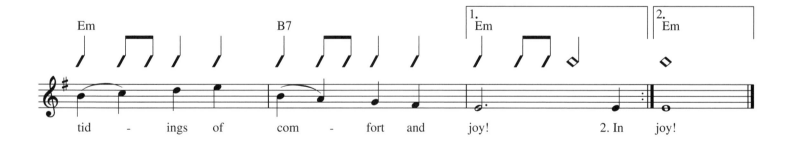

tid - ings of com - fort and joy! 2. In joy!

Additional Lyrics

2. In Bethlehem, in Jewry
   This blessed babe was born
   And laid within a manger
   Upon this blessed morn
   To which His mother Mary
   Did nothing take in scorn.

Good King Wenceslas

Words by John M. Neale
Music from Piae Cantiones

Additional Lyrics

2. "Hither page, and stand by me,
   If thou know'st it, telling;
   Yonder peasant, who is he?
   Where and what his dwelling?"
   "Sire, he lives a good league hence,
   Underneath the mountain;
   Right against the forest fence,
   By Saint Agnes' fountain."

3. "Bring me flesh, and bring me wine,
   Bring me pine-logs hither;
   Thou and I will see him dine,
   When we bear them thither."
   Page and monarch forth they went,
   Forth they went together;
   Through the rude winds wild lament,
   And the bitter weather.

4. "Sire, the night is darker now,
   And the wind blows stronger;
   Fails my heart, I know not how,
   I can go not longer."
   "Mark my footsteps, my good page,
   Tread thou in them boldly:
   Thou shalt find the winter's rage
   Freeze thy blood less coldly."

5. In his master's steps he trod,
   Where the snow lay dinted;
   Heat was in the very sod
   Which the saint has printed.
   Therefore, Christian men, be sure,
   Wealth or rank possessing;
   Ye who now will bless the poor,
   Shall yourselves find blessing.

Grandma Got Run Over by a Reindeer

Words and Music by Randy Brooks

Chorus
Moderately Bright

Grand-ma got run o-ver by a rein-deer walk-ing home from our house Christ-mas Eve. You can say there's no such thing as San-ta, but as for me and Grand-pa, we be-lieve.

To Coda ⊕   **Verse**

1. She'd been drink-ing too much
2., 3. *See Additional Lyrics*

egg-nog and we begged her not to go. But she for-got her med-i-ca-tion, and she stag-gered out the door in-to the

snow. When we found her Christ-mas morn-ing

at the scene of the at-tack, she had hoof-prints on her

fore-head, and in-crim-i-nat-ing Claus marks on her back. elves.

Coda

Outro-Chorus

lieve. Grand-ma got run o-ver by a rein-deer

walk-ing home from our house Christ-mas Eve. You can say there's no such thing as

San-ta, but as for me and Grand-pa, we be-lieve.

Additional Lyrics

2. Now we're all so proud of Grandpa.
   He's been taking it so well.
   See him in there watching football,
   Drinking beer and playing cards with Cousin Mel.
   It's not Christmas without Grandma.
   All the family's dressed in black,
   And we just can't help but wonder:
   Should we open up her gifts or send them back?

3. Now the goose is on the table,
   And the pudding made of fig.
   And the blue and silver candles,
   That would just have matched the hair in Grandma's wig.
   I've warned all my friends and neighbors.
   Better watch out for yourselves.
   They should never give a license
   To a man who drives a sleigh and plays with elves.

Grandma's Killer Fruitcake

Words and Music by Elmo Shropshire and Rita Abrams

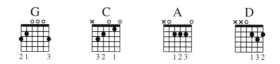

Intro
Country Polka

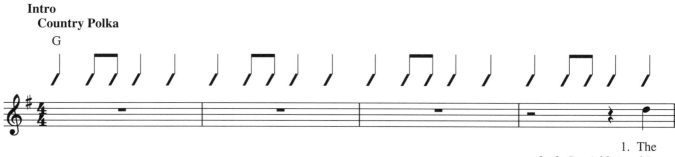

1. The
2., 3. *See Additional Lyrics*

Verse

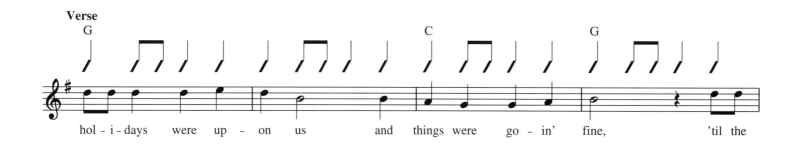

hol - i - days were up - on us and things were go - in' fine, 'til the

day I heard the door - bell and a chill ran up my spine. I

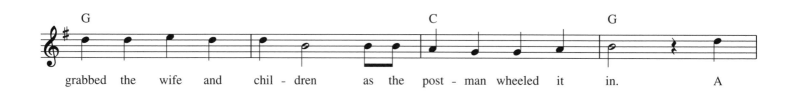

grabbed the wife and chil - dren as the post - man wheeled it in. A

year - ly Christ - mas night - mare has just come back a - gain. It was

Chorus

hard - er than the head of Un - cle Buck - y, heav - y as a Ser - mon of

Preach - er Luck - y. One's e - nough to give the whole state of Ken - tuck - y a

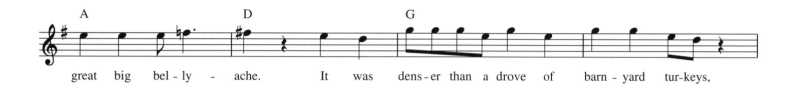

great big bel - ly - ache. It was dens - er than a drove of barn - yard tur-keys,

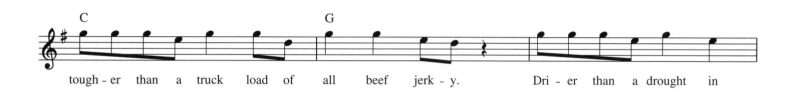

tough - er than a truck load of all beef jerk - y. Dri - er than a drought in

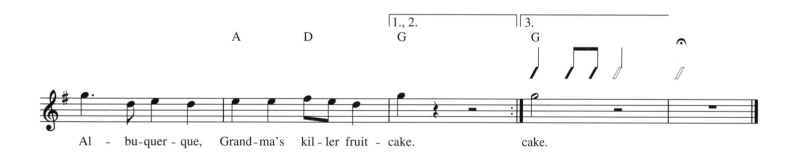

Al - bu-quer - que, Grand-ma's kil - ler fruit - cake. cake.

Additional Lyrics

2. Now I've had to swallow some marginal fare at our family feast.
I even downed Aunt Dolly's possom pie just to keep the family peace.
I winced at Wilma's gizzard mousse, but said it tasted fine,
But that lethal weapon that Grandma bakes is where I draw the line.

3. It's early Christmas morning, the phone rings us awake.
It's Grandma, Pa, she wants to know how'd we like the cake.
"Well, Grandma, I never. Uh, we couldn't. It was, uh, unbelievable, that's for shore.
What's that you say? Oh, no Grandma, Puh-leez don't send us more!"

The Greatest Gift of All

Words and Music by John Jarvis

Through the win - dow I __ can see __ snow be - gin to fall.

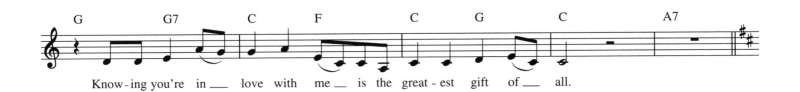

Know-ing you're in __ love with me __ is the great - est gift of __ all.

Verse

3. Just be - fore I go to sleep ____ I hear a church bell ring.

Mer - ry Christ - mas ev - 'ry - one ____ is the song it ____ sings.

So I say a si - lent prayer ____ for crea - tures great and small.

Peace on earth good _ will to men is the great - est gift of __ all. Peace on earth good _

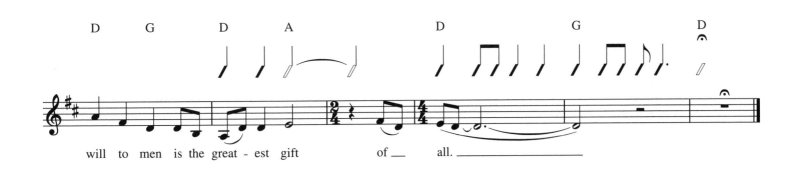

will to men is the great - est gift of __ all. _____

Happy Holiday

from the Motion Picture Irving Berlin's HOLIDAY INN

Words and Music by Irving Berlin

Hark! The Herald Angels Sing

Words by Charles Wesley
Altered by George Whitefield
Music by Felix Mendelssohn-Bärtholdy

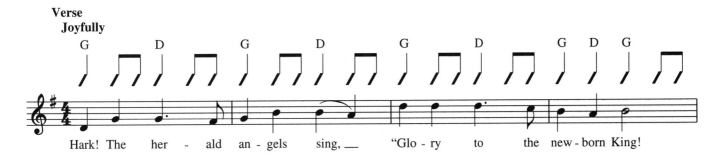

Verse
Joyfully

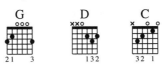

Hark! The her - ald an - gels sing, ___ "Glo - ry to the new - born King!

Peace on earth, and mer - cy mild, ___ God and sin - ners re - con - ciled."

Chorus

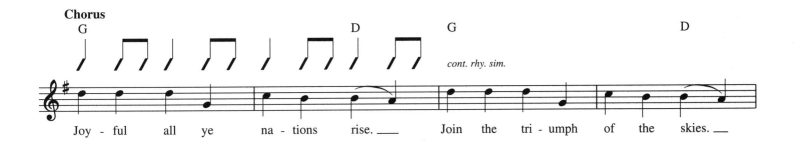

Joy - ful all ye na - tions rise. ___ Join the tri - umph of the skies. ___

With th'an - gel - ic host pro - claim, "Christ is ___ born in Beth - le - hem."

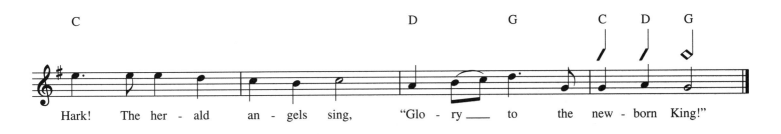

Hark! The her - ald an - gels sing, "Glo - ry ___ to the new - born King!"

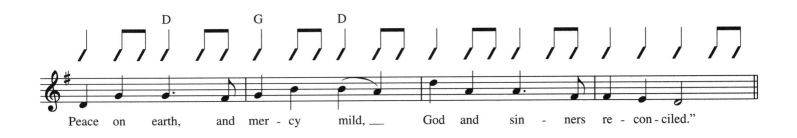

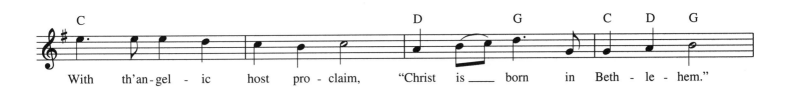

Happy Xmas (War Is Over)

Words and Music by John Lennon and Yoko Ono

A Holly Jolly Christmas

Music and Lyrics by Johnny Marks

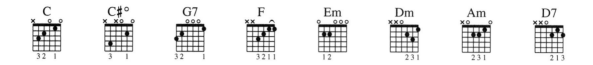

1. Have a (4.) hol - ly jol - ly Christ - mas, it's the best time of the

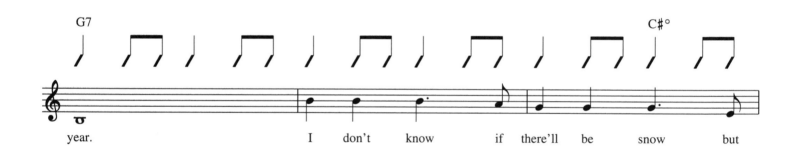

year. I don't know if there'll be snow but

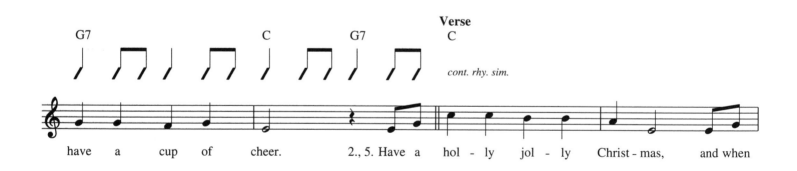

have a cup of cheer. 2., 5. Have a hol - ly jol - ly Christ - mas, and when

you walk down the street, say hel - lo to friends you know and

Bridge

G7 · · C · F · Em

ev - 'ry - one you meet. Oh, ho, the mis - tle - toe

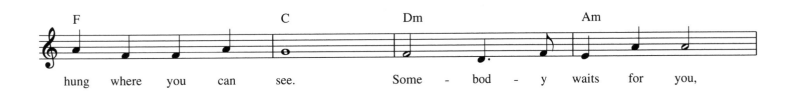

F · C · Dm · Am

hung where you can see. Some - bod - y waits for you,

Verse

D7 · G7 · C

kiss her once for me. 3., 6. Have a hol - ly jol - ly Christ - mas, and in

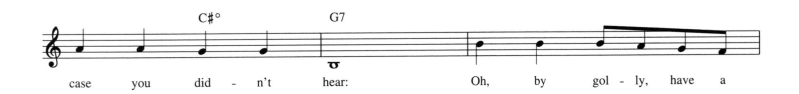

C#° · G7

case you did - n't hear: Oh, by gol - ly, have a

1.

C · D7 · G7 · C

hol - ly jol - ly Christ - mas this year. 4. Have a

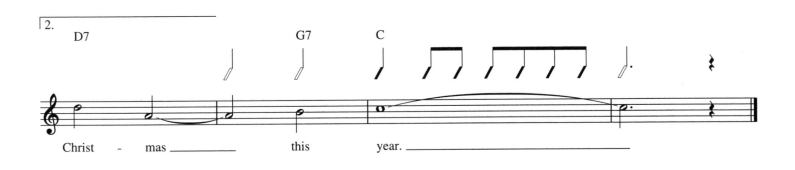

2.

D7 · G7 · C

Christ - mas _____ this year. _____

(There's No Place Like)
Home for the Holidays

Words by Al Stillman
Music by Robert Allen

Hymne

By Vangelis

I Heard the Bells on Christmas Day

Words by Henry Wadsworth Longfellow
Music by John Baptiste Calkin

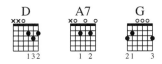

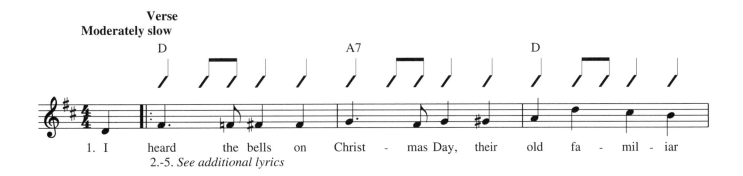

Verse
Moderately slow

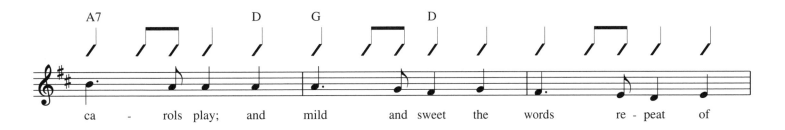

1. I heard the bells on Christ - mas Day, their old fa - mil - iar
2.-5. *See additional lyrics*

ca - rols play; and mild and sweet the words re - peat of

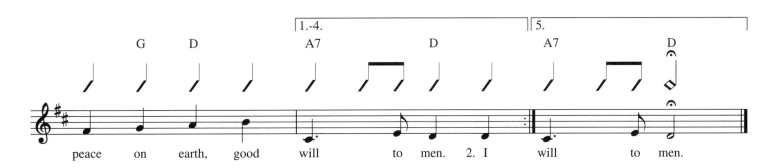

peace on earth, good will to men. 2. I will to men.

Additional Lyrics

2. I thought as now this day had come,
   The belfries of all Christendom
   Had rung so long the unbroken song
   Of peace on earth, good will to men.

3. And in despair I bow'd my head:
   "There is no peace on earth," I said,
   "For hate is strong, and mocks the song
   Of peace on earth, good will to men."

4. Then pealed the bells more loud and deep:
   "God is not dead, nor doth He sleep;
   The wrong shall fail, the right prevail,
   With peace on earth, good will to men."

5. Till ringing, singing on it's way,
   The world revolved from night to day,
   Avoice, a chime, a chant sublime,
   Of peace on earth, good will to men!"

I Saw Mommy Kissing Santa Claus

Words and Music by Tommie Connor

I Saw Three Ships

Traditional English Carol

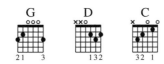

1. I saw three ships come sail - ing in, on Christ - mas Day, on
2. *See additional lyrics*

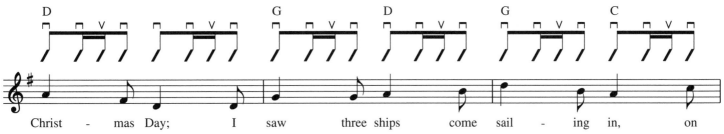

Christ - mas Day; I saw three ships come sail - ing in, on

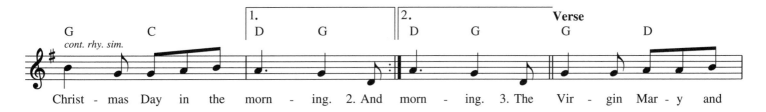

Christ - mas Day in the morn - ing. 2. And morn - ing. 3. The Vir - gin Mar - y and

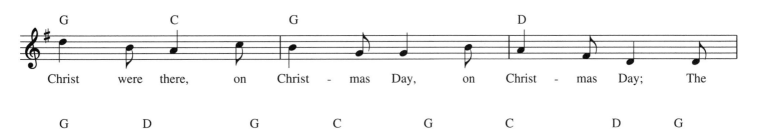

Christ were there, on Christ - mas Day, on Christ - mas Day; The

Vir - gin Mar - y and Christ were there, on Christ - mas Day in the morn - ing.

Additional Lyrics

2. And what was in those ships, all three,
On Christmas Day, on Christmas Day;
And what was in those ships, all three,
On Christmas Day in the morning.

I'll Be Home for Christmas

Words and Music by Kim Gannon and Walter Kent

It Came Upon the Midnight Clear

Words by Edmund H. Sears
Traditional English Melody
Adapted by Arthur Sullivan

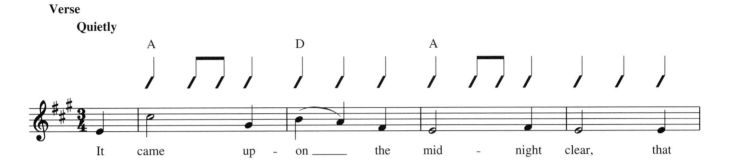

Verse
Quietly

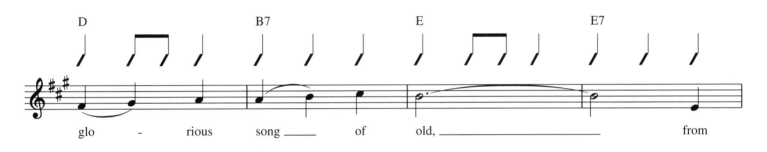

It came up-on ___ the mid-night clear, that

glo-rious song ___ of old, _____ from

an-gels bend-ing near the earth to touch their harps ___ of

Chorus

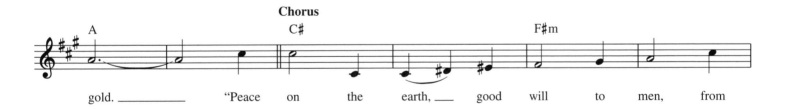

gold. _____ "Peace on the earth, ___ good will to men, from

heaven's ___ all gra-cious King." _____ The world in sol-emn

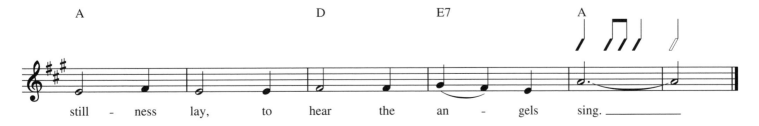

still-ness lay, to hear the an-gels sing. _____

I'm Spending Christmas With You

Words and Music by Tom Occhipinti

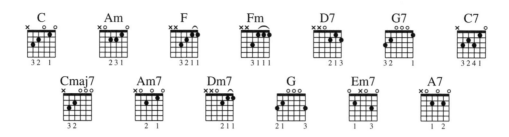

Verse

Moderately Slow

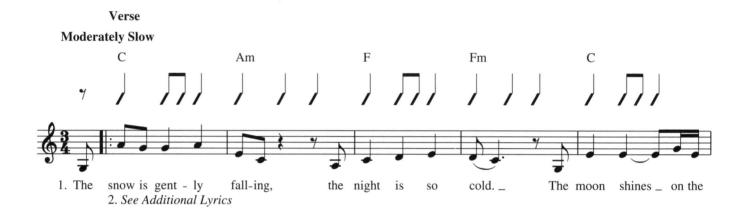

1. The snow is gent-ly fall-ing, the night is so cold. _ The moon shines _ on the
2. *See Additional Lyrics*

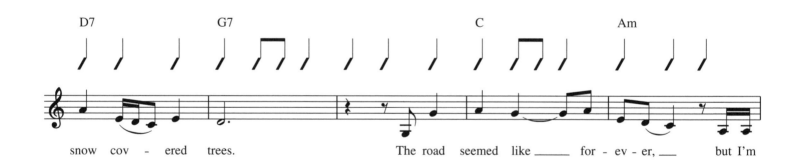

snow cov-ered trees. The road seemed like _____ for-ev-er, ___ but I'm

fi-nal-ly home. _ We're a-lone on this Christ-mas Eve.

%. Chorus

I'm spend - ing Christ - mas _____ with ____ you. _____ 'Tis the

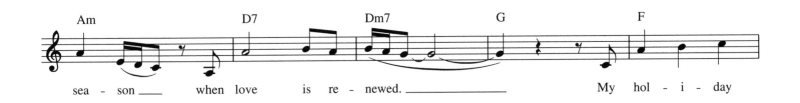

sea - son ____ when love is re - newed. _____ My hol - i - day

To Coda ⊕

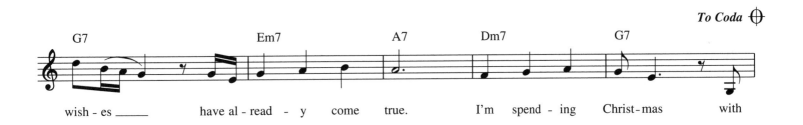

wish - es _____ have al - read - y come true. I'm spend - ing Christ - mas with

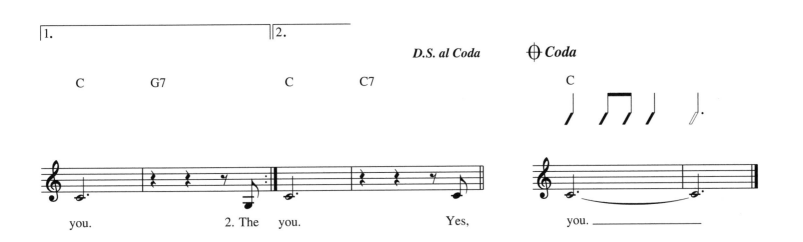

you.   2. The you.   Yes,   you. _____

Additional Lyrics

2. The fireplace is burning and your hands feel so warm.
   We're hanging popcorn on the tree.
   I take you in my arms, your lips touch mine.
   It feels like our first Christmas Eve.

I've Got My Love to Keep Me Warm

from the 20th Century Fox Motion Picture ON THE AVENUE
Words and Music by Irving Berlin

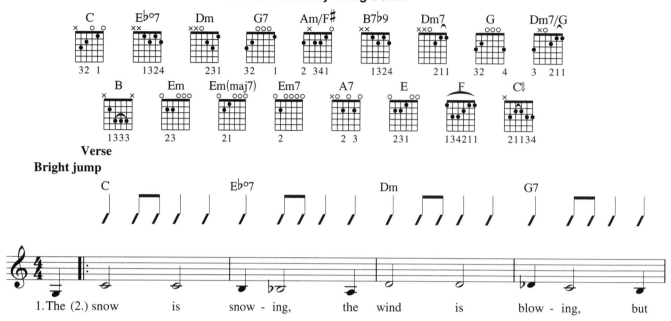

Verse
Bright jump

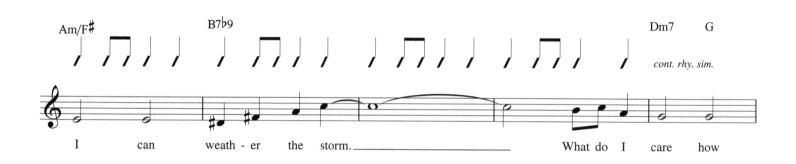

1.The (2.) snow   is   snow - ing,   the   wind   is   blow - ing,   but

I   can   weath - er   the   storm._____   What   do   I   care   how

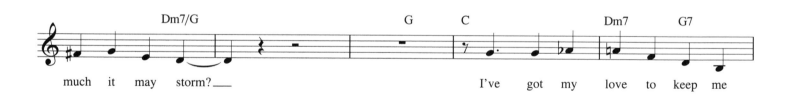

much   it   may   storm?___   I've   got   my   love   to   keep   me

warm._____   I   can't   re - mem - ber   a   worse   De - cem - ber;   just

watch   those   i - ci - cles   form._____   What do   I   care   if   i - ci - cles   form?___

I've got my love to keep me warm.

Bridge

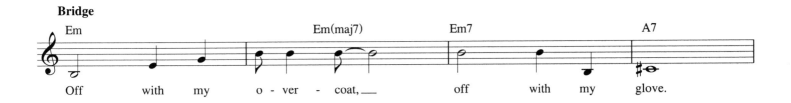

Off with my o - ver - coat, ___ off with my glove.

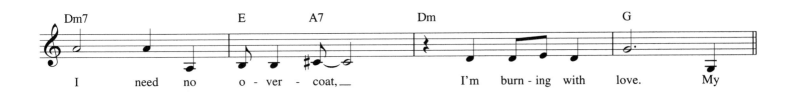

I need no o - ver - coat, ___ I'm burn - ing with love. My

Outro-Verse

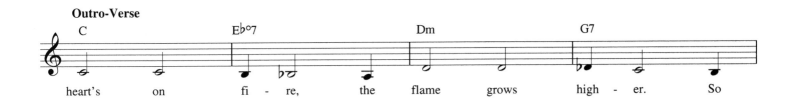

heart's on fi - re, the flame grows high - er. So

I will weath - er the storm. ___ What do I care how

much it may storm? ___ I've got my

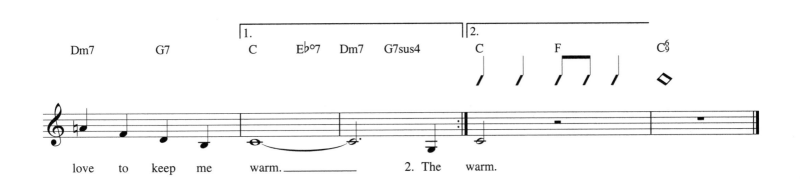

love to keep me warm. ___ 2. The warm.

It Must Have Been the Mistletoe
(Our First Christmas)
By Justin Wilde and Doug Konecky

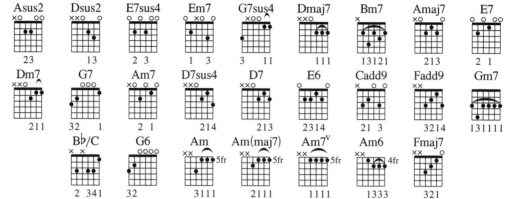

Verse

Moderately

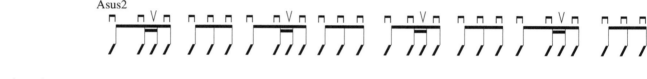

1. It must have been the mis-tle-toe, the la-zy fire, the fall-ing snow, the

ma-gic in the frost-y air, that feel-ing ev-'ry-where. It

must have been the pret-ty lights that glis-tened in the si-lent night, or

Bridge

may-be just the stars so bright that shined a-bove you. Our first Christ-mas,

more than _ we'd been dream - ing of._____ Old Saint Nich - 'las

had his fin - gers crossed, that we would fall in love. _ 2. It

Verse

could have been _ the hol - i - day, _ the mid-night ride _ up - on a sleigh, _ the

coun - try - side _ all dressed in white, _ that cra - zy snow - ball fight. It

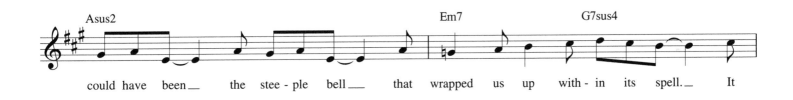

could have been _ the stee - ple bell _ that wrapped us up with - in its spell. _ It

on - ly took one kiss to know, _ it must have been the

Bridge

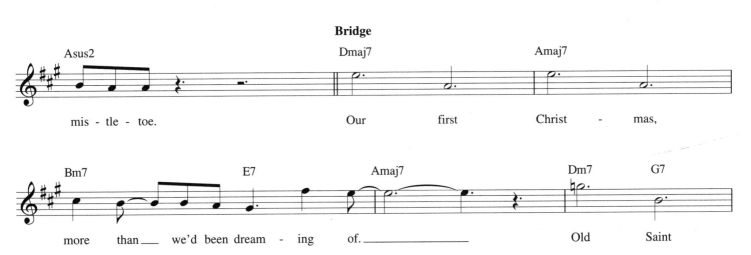

mis - tle - toe. Our first Christ - mas,

more than _ we'd been dream - ing of. _____ Old Saint

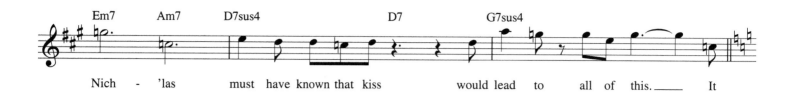

Em7   Am7   D7sus4   D7   G7sus4

Nich - 'las   must have known that kiss   would lead to   all of this.____   It

Outro-Verse

Cadd9

must have been____   the mis - tle - toe,____   the la - zy fire,____   the fall - ing snow,_   the

Fadd9   G7sus4

mag - ic in____   the frost - y air,____   that made   me   love   you.   On

Cadd9   Gm7   B♭/C

Christ - mas Eve____   a wish come true,_   that night I____   fell in love with you.____   It

Fadd9   Dm7   G7sus4

on - ly took____   one kiss to know,_   it must   have   been   the

Cadd9   Dm7   G6   Am   Am(maj7) Am7ᵛ Am6

mis - tle - toe!   It must   have   been   the mis - tle - toe!   It

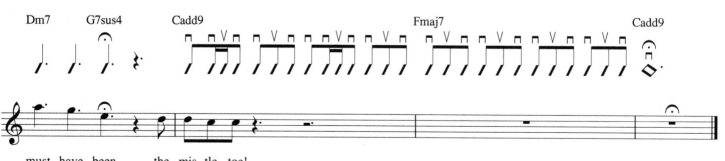

Dm7   G7sus4   Cadd9   Fmaj7   Cadd9

must have been   the mis - tle - toe!

It's Beginning to Look Like Christmas

By Meredith Willson

%% Verse

Brightly

1. It's be-(2.) gin-ning to look a lot like Christ-mas, ev - 'ry-where you go. { Take a / There's a

look in the five and ten, glis-ten-ing once a-gain with can-dy canes and sil-ver lanes a - glow. } It's be-
tree in the grand ho-tel, one in the park, as well; the stur-dy kind that does-n't mind the snow.

cont. rhy. sim.

gin-ning to look a - lot like Christ - mas, { toys in ev - 'ry store. But the / soon the bells will start. And the

To Coda ⊕

pret - ti-est sight to see is the hol - ly that will be, on your own front door. A pair of
thing that will make them ring is the ca - rol that you sing right with - in your

Bridge

hop - a - long boots and a pis - tol that shoots is the wish of Bar - ney and Ben.

Dolls that will talk and will go for a walk is the hope of Jan - ice and Jen. And

D.S. al Coda

⊕ Coda

Mom and Dad can hard - ly wait for school to start a - gain. 2. It's be - heart.

It's Christmas in New York

Words and Music by Billy Butt

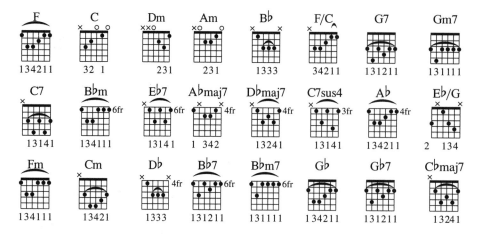

Verse
Moderately

1. Church-bells are ring-ing,_____ choirs__ are sing-ing,_____
2. Rest-'rant signs sway-ing,_____ blue skies are gray-ing,_____

joy they are bring-ing,_____ it's Christ-mas in New York.
ev-'ry-one's say-ing,_____ it's Christ-mas in New York.

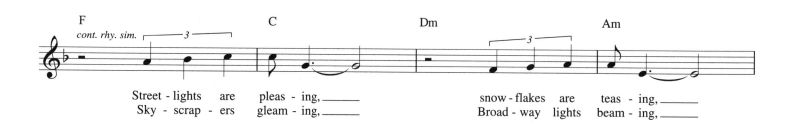

Street - lights are pleas-ing,_____ snow-flakes are teas-ing,_____
Sky - scrap - ers gleam-ing,_____ Broad-way lights beam-ing,_____

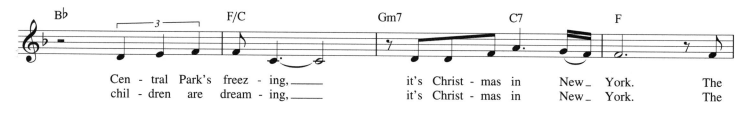

Cen - tral Park's freez - ing,_____ it's Christ - mas in New_ York. The
chil - dren are dream - ing,_____ it's Christ - mas in New_ York. The

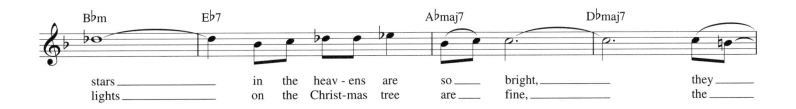

stars _____ in the heav - ens are so _____ bright, _____ they _____
lights _____ on the Christ-mas tree are ____ fine, _____ the _____

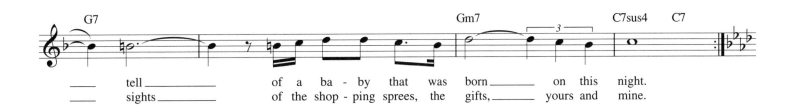

_____ tell _____ of a ba - by that was born _____ on this night.
_____ sights _____ of the shop - ping sprees, the gifts, _____ yours and mine.

Verse

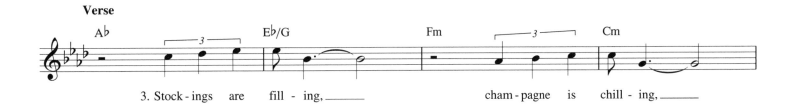

3. Stock - ings are fill - ing, _____ cham - pagne is chill - ing, _____

it's all so thrill - ing _____ it's Christ-mas in New York.

Log fires are burn - ing, _____ San - ta's re - turn - ing _____

fill - ing each yearn - ing, _____ it's Christ-mas in New _ York.

Interlude

Outro-Verse

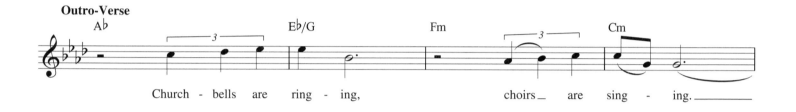

Church - bells are ring - ing, choirs — are sing - ing. _____

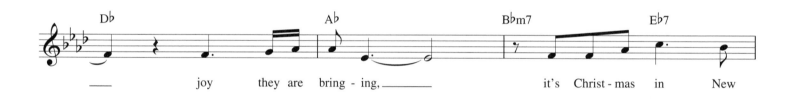

_____ joy they are bring - ing, _____ it's Christ - mas in New

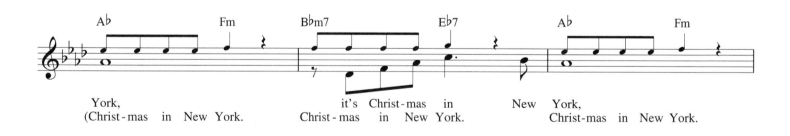

York, it's Christ - mas in New York,
(Christ - mas in New York. Christ - mas in New York. Christ - mas in New York.

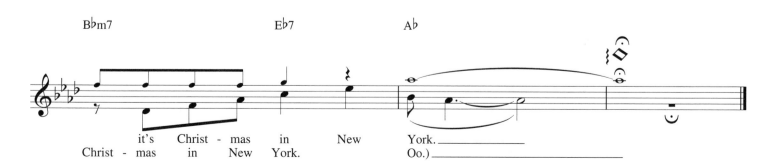

it's Christ - mas in New York. _____
Christ - mas in New York. Oo.) _____

Jesus Is Born

Words and Music by Steve Green, Phil Naish and Colleen Green

Christ has fi - nal - ly come. Glo - ry to ___ the King, let the peo - ple sing

Hal - le - lu - jah, ___ Hal - le - lu - jah. ___

Verse

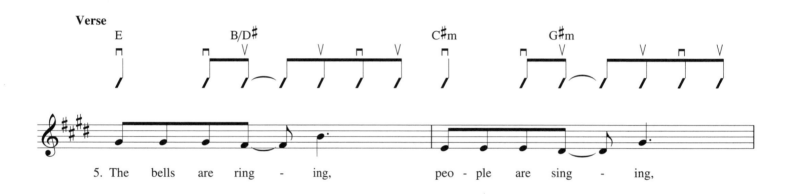

5. The bells are ring - ing, peo - ple are sing - ing,

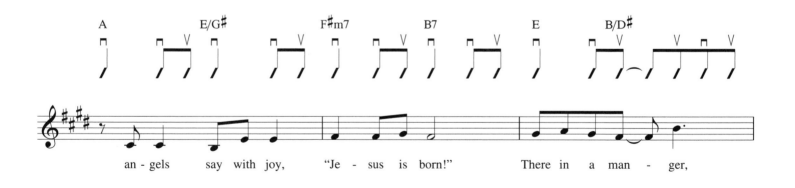

an - gels say with joy, "Je - sus is born!" There in a man - ger,

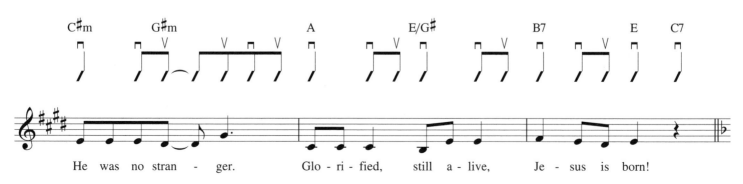

He was no stran - ger. Glo - ri - fied, still a - live, Je - sus is born!

Verse

The bells are ring - ing, peo - ple are sing - ing, an - gels say with joy,

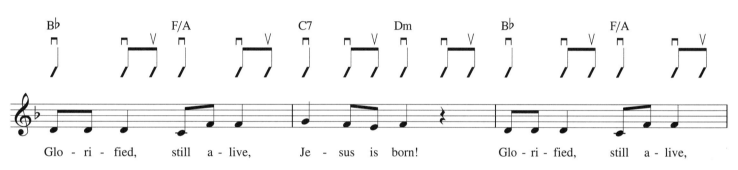

"Je - sus is born!" There in a man - ger, He was no stran - ger.

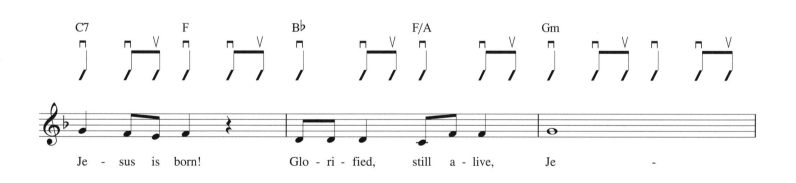

Glo - ri - fied, still a - live, Je - sus is born! Glo - ri - fied, still a - live,

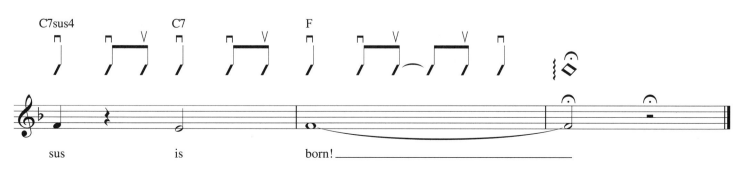

Je - sus is born! Glo - ri - fied, still a - live, Je -

sus is born!

Jingle-Bell Rock

Words and Music by Joe Beal and Jim Boothe

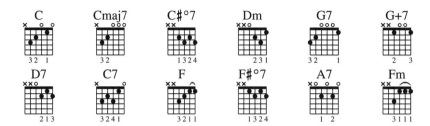

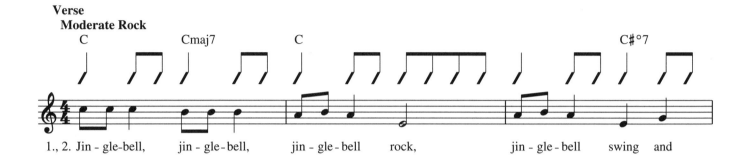

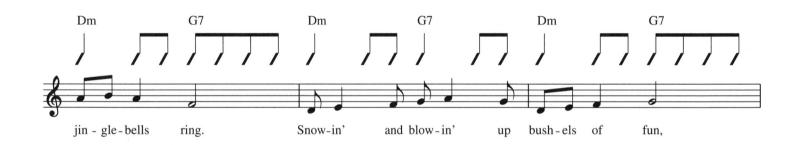

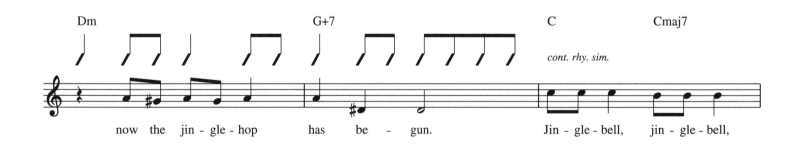

Jin - gle - bell Square   in the fros - ty air.   What a bright time, it's the

right   time   to   rock   the   night   a - way.   Jin - gle - bell   time   is   a

swell   time   to   go   gli - din'   in   a   one   horse   sleigh.

Outro

Gid - dy - ap,   jin - gle horse   pick up   your feet,   jin - gle a - round   the   clock.

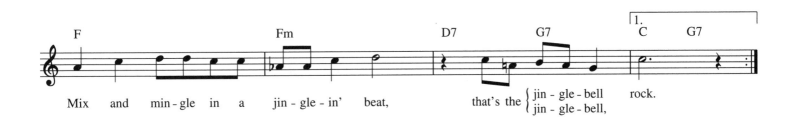

Mix   and   min - gle   in   a   jin - gle - in'   beat,   that's the ⎰ jin - gle - bell   rock.
                                                                                        ⎱ jin - gle - bell,

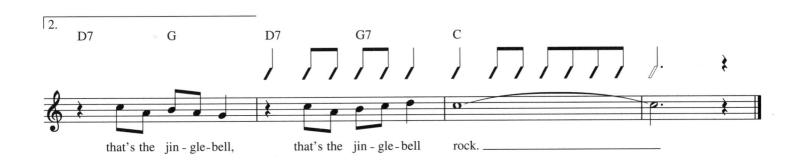

that's the   jin - gle - bell,   that's the   jin - gle - bell   rock. _____

Jingle Bells

Words and Music by J. Pierpont

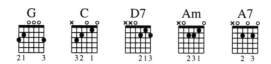

Verse
Brightly

1. Dash - ing through the snow, in a one horse o - pen sleigh.
2., 3. *See Additional Lyrics*

O'er the fields we go, laugh - ing all the way.

cont. rhy. sim.

Bells on bob - tail ring, mak - ing spir - its bright. What

fun it is to ride and sing a sleigh - ing song to - night! Oh!

Chorus

Jin - gle bells, jin - gle bells, jin - gle all the way.

Oh, what fun it is to ride in a one horse o - pen sleigh! _____

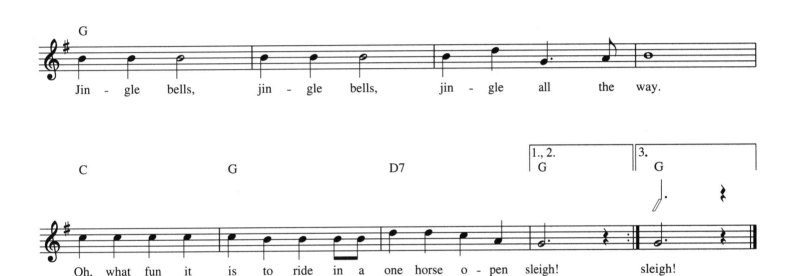

Jin - gle bells, jin - gle bells, jin - gle all the way.

Oh, what fun it is to ride in a one horse o - pen sleigh! sleigh!

Additional lyrics

2. A day or two ago, I thought I'd take a ride,
   And soon Miss Fannie Bright was sitting by my side.
   The horse was lean and lank,
   Misfortune seemed his lot.
   He got into a drifted bank and we, we got upshot! Oh!

3. Now the ground is white, go it while you're young.
   Take the girls tonight and sing this sleighing song.
   Just get a bobtail bay,
   Two-forty for his speed.
   Then hitch him to an open sleigh and
   Crack, you'll take the lead! Oh!

Jolly Old St. Nicholas

Traditional 19th Century American Carol

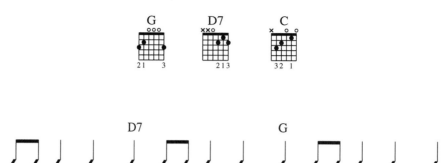

Verse
Brightly

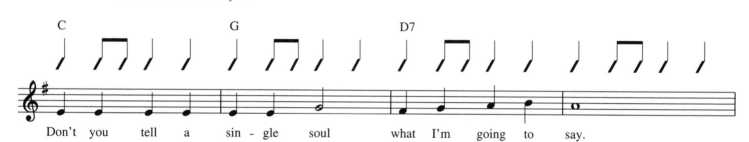

1. Jol - ly old Saint Nich - o - las, lean your ear this way.
2., 3. *See additional lyrics*

Don't you tell a sin - gle soul what I'm going to say.

cont. rhy. sim.

Christ - mas Eve is com - ing soon, now, you dear old man,

whis - per what you'll bring to me; tell me if you can. best.

Additional Lyrics

2. When the clock is striking twelve, when I'm fast asleep.
   Down the chimney broad and black, with your pack you'll creep.
   All the stockings you will find hanging in a row.
   Mine will be the shortest one, you'll be sure to know.

3. Johnny wants a pair of skates; Susy wants a sled.
   Nellie wants a picture book, yellow, blue and red.
   Now I think I'll leave to you what to give the rest.
   Choose for me, dear Santa Claus.
   You will know the best.

Joy to the World

Words by Isaac Watts
Music by George Frideric Handel
Arranged by Lowell Mason

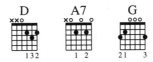

Additional Lyrics

2. He rules the world with truth and grace
   And makes the nations prove
   The glories of His righteousness
   And wonders of His love,
   And wonders of His love.
   And wonders, wonders of His love.

Last Christmas

Words and Music by George Michael

_____ love you." I meant it. Now___ I know___ what a fool_____ I've been.___ But if you

kissed me now___ I know you'd fool me a - gain.___ fool me a - gain.___

$\oplus$ **Coda**   **Verse**

- cial.   3. A   face   on a lov - er with a   fire   in   his   heart,___   a

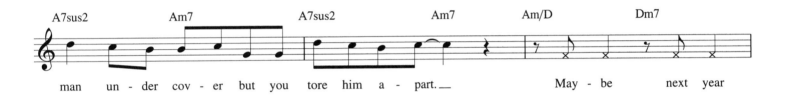

man un - der cov - er but you tore him a - part.___   May - be   next year

I'll give it to some - one, I'll give it to some - one spe -

Outro

- cial,   spe - cial._____   Some-one,_____

Repeat and fade

some - one.   I'll give it to some - one, I'll give it to some - one spe -

Additional Lyrics

2. A crowded room, friends with tired eyes.
   I'm hiding from you and your soul of ice.
   My God, I thought you were someone to rely on.
   Me, I guess I was a shoulder to cry on.
   A face on a lover with a fire in his heart,
   A man undercover but you tore me apart.
   Ooh, now I've found a real love.
   You'll never fool me again.

Let It Snow! Let It Snow! Let It Snow!

Words by Sammy Cahn
Music by Jule Styne

A Marshmallow World

Words by Carl Sigman
Music by Peter De Rose

Little Saint Nick

Words and Music by Brian Wilson and Mike Love

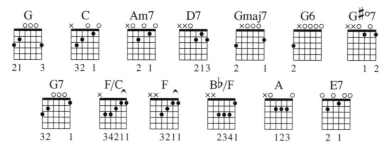

Tune down ½ step:
(low to high) Eb - Ab - Db - Gb - Bb - Eb

Intro
Moderately fast

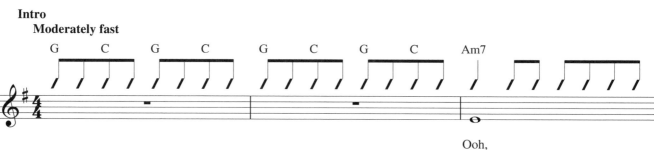

Ooh,

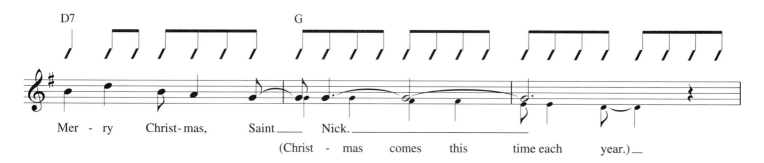

Mer - ry   Christ - mas,   Saint ___ Nick. _____
(Christ - mas   comes   this   time   each   year.) ___

% Verse

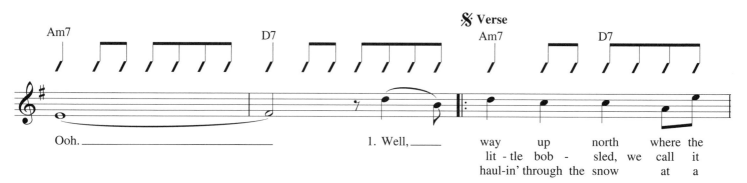

Ooh. _____   1. Well, ___   way   up   north   where   the
lit - tle   bob - sled,   we   call   it
haul - in' through the   snow   at   a

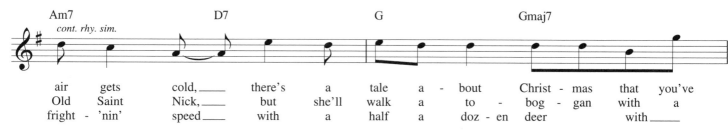

air   gets   cold, ___   there's   a   tale   a - bout   Christ - mas   that   you've
Old   Saint   Nick, ___   but   she'll   walk   a   to - bog - gan   with   a
fright - 'nin'   speed ___   with   a   half   a   doz - en   deer   with ___

all   been   told. ___   And   a   real   fa - mous   cat   all   dressed
four - speed   stick. ___   She's   can - dy   ap - ple   red   with   a
Ru - dy   to   lead.   He's   got - ta   wear   his   gog - gles 'cause the

Merry Christmas, Darling

Words and Music by Richard Carpenter and Frank Pooler

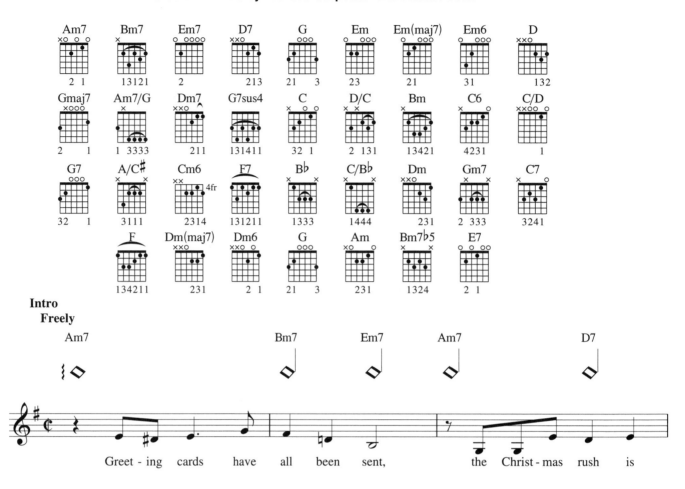

Intro
Freely

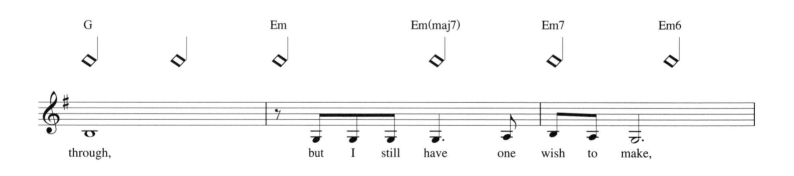

Greet-ing cards have all been sent, the Christ-mas rush is through, but I still have one wish to make,

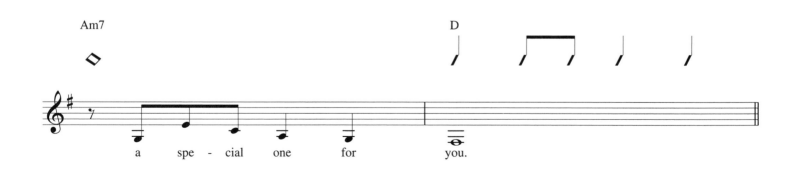

a spe-cial one for you.

Verse

Moderately slow

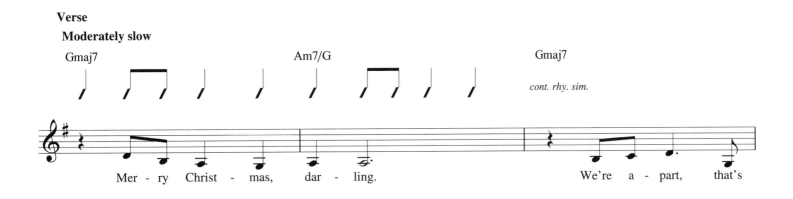

cont. rhy. sim.

Mer - ry Christ - mas, dar - ling. We're a - part, that's

true; but I can dream and in my dreams, I'm

Christ - mas - ing with you. Hol - i - days are joy - ful,

there's al - ways some - thing new. But ev - 'ry day's a hol - i - day

𝄋 Bridge

when I'm near to you. The ___ lights on my tree I

wish you could see, I wish it ev - 'ry day. The

logs on the fire   fill me with de - sire   to see you and to ___

Outro-Verse

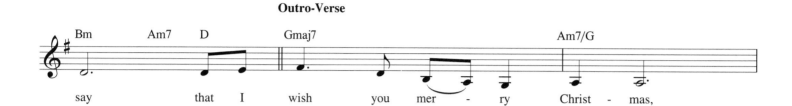

say   that I wish   you mer - ry Christ - mas,

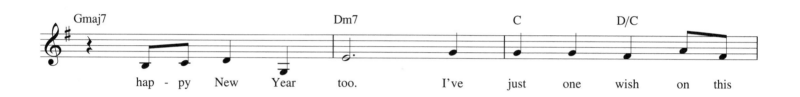

hap - py New Year too.   I've just one wish on this

To Coda 𝄌   *D.S. al Coda*

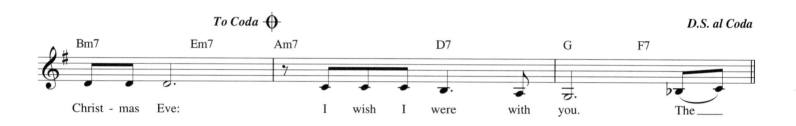

Christ - mas Eve: I wish I were with you.   The ___

𝄌 **Coda**

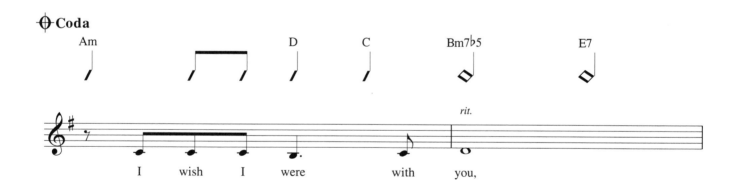

I wish I were with you,

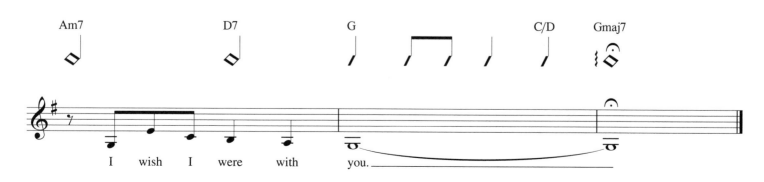

I wish I were with you. ___

O Christmas Tree

Traditional German Carol

Additional Lyrics

2. O, Christmas tree! O, Christmas tree,
   Much pleasure doth thou bring me!
   O, Christmas tree! O, Christmas tree,
   Much pleasure does thou bring me!
   For every year the Christmas tree
   Brings to us all both joy and glee.
   O, Christmas tree, O, Christmas tree,
   Much pleasure doth thou bring me!

3. O, Christmas tree! O, Christmas tree,
   Thy candles shine out brightly!
   O, Christmas tree, O, Christmas tree,
   Thy candles shine out brightly!
   Each bough doth hold its tiny light
   That makes each toy to sparkle bright.
   O, Christmas tree, O, Christmas tree,
   Thy candles shine out brightly.

The Most Wonderful Time of the Year

Words and Music by Eddie Pola and George Wyle

Bridge

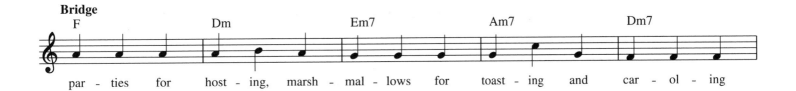

par - ties for host - ing, marsh - mal - lows for toast - ing and car - ol - ing

out in the snow. There'll be scar - y ghost stor - ies and

D.S. al Coda

tales of the glo - ries of Christ - mas - es long, long a - go. _____ 3. It's the

Coda
Outro

most won - der - ful time, it's the most won - der - ful

time. It's the most won - der - ful time _____

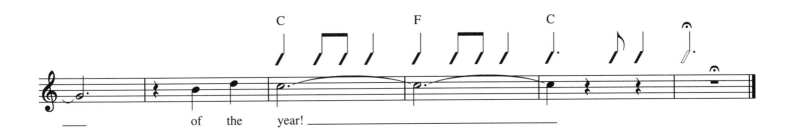

_____ of the year! _____

Additional Lyrics

2. It's the hap-happiest season of all,
   With those holiday greetings
   And gay happy meetings
   When friends come to call.
   It's the hap-happiest season of all.

3. It's the most wonderful time of the year.
   There'll be much mistletoeing
   And hearts will be glowing
   When loved ones are near.
   It's the most wonderful time of the year.

My Favorite Things

from THE SOUND OF MUSIC

Lyrics by Oscar Hammerstein II
Music by Richard Rodgers

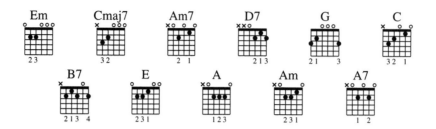

Verse
Lively, With Spirit

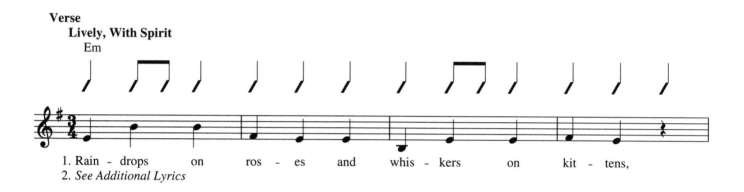

1. Rain - drops on ros - es and whis - kers on kit - tens,
2. *See Additional Lyrics*

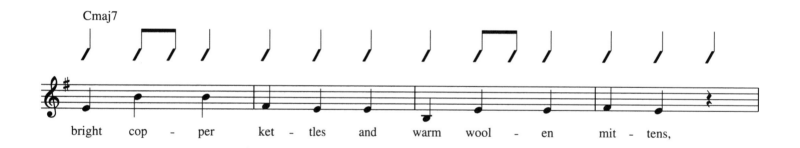

bright cop - per ket - tles and warm wool - en mit - tens,

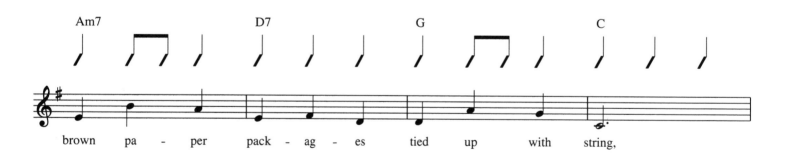

brown pa - per pack - ag - es tied up with string,

these are a few of my fa - vor - ite things.

Verse

3. Girls in white dress - es with blue sat - in sash - es, snow - flakes that stay on my nose and eye - lash - es, sil - ver white win - ters that melt in - to springs, these are a few of my fa - vor - ite

Outro

things. When the dog bites, when the bee stings, when I'm feel - ing sad, _____ I sim - ply re - mem - ber my fa - vor - ite things and then I don't feel

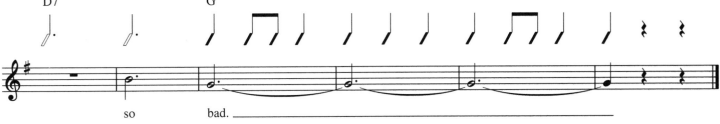

so bad. _____

Additional Lyrics

2. Cream colored ponies and crisp apple strudles,
Doorbells and sleigh bells and schnitzel with noodles,
Wild geese that fly with the moon on their wings,
These are a few of my favorite things.

The Night Before Christmas Song

Music by Johnny Marks
Lyrics adapted by Johnny Marks from Clement Moore's Poem

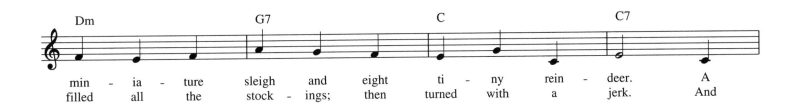

min - ia - ture sleigh and eight ti - ny rein - deer. A
filled all the stock - ings; then turned with a jerk. And

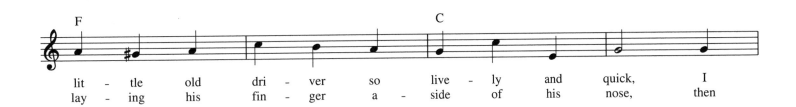

lit - tle old dri - ver so live - ly and quick, I
lay - ing his fin - ger a - side of his nose, then

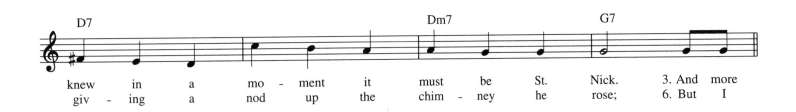

knew in a mo - ment it must be St. Nick. 3. And more
giv - ing a nod up the chim - ney he rose; 6. But I

Verse

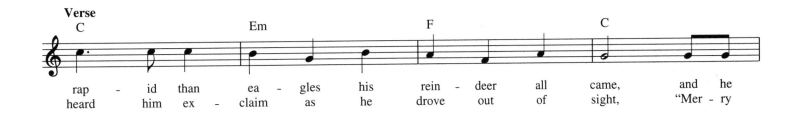

rap - id than ea - gles his rein - deer all came, and he
heard him ex - claim as he drove out of sight, "Mer - ry

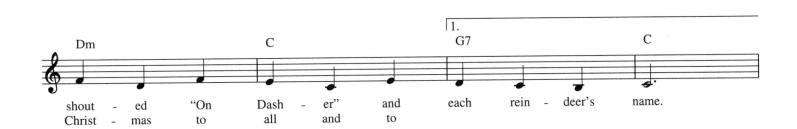

shout - ed "On Dash - er" and each rein - deer's name.
Christ - mas to all and and to

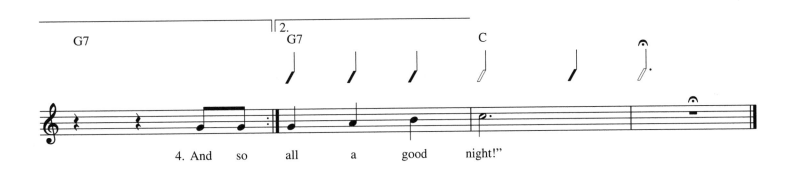

4. And so all a good night!"

Nuttin' for Christmas

Words and Music by Roy Bennett and Sid Tepper

Chorus

I'm get - tin' nut - tin' for Christ - mas. Mom - my and

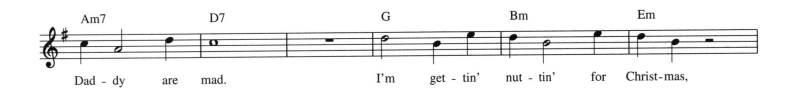

Dad - dy are mad. I'm get - tin' nut - tin' for Christ-mas,

'cause I ain't been nut - tin' but bad. _____ 2. I

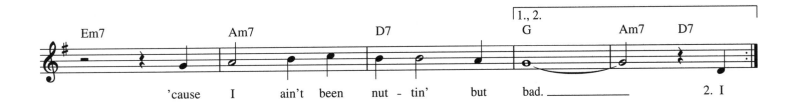

Outro

bad. _____ So you bet - ter be good, what - ev - er you do, 'cause if you're bad I'm

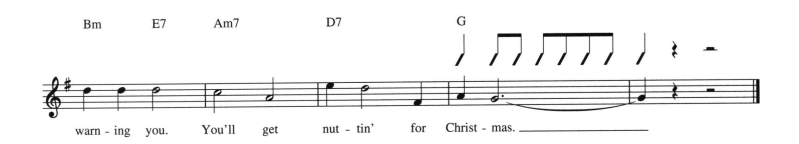

warn - ing you. You'll get nut - tin' for Christ - mas. _____

Additional Lyrics

2. I put a tack on teacher's chair;
   Somebody snitched on me.
   I tied a knot in Susie's hair;
   Somebody snitched on me.
   I did a dance on Mommy's plants,
   Climbed a tree and tore my pants.
   Filled the sugar bowl with ants;
   Somebody snitched on me.

3. I won't be seeing Santa Claus;
   Somebody snitched on me.
   He won't come visit me because
   Somebody snitched on me.
   Next year, I'll be going straight.
   Next year, I'll be good, just wait.
   I'd start now but it's too late;
   Somebody snitched on me.

O Come, All Ye Faithful
(Adeste Fideles)

Words and Music by John Francis Wade
Latin Words translated by Frederick Oakeley

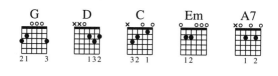

Additional Lyrics

2. Sing choirs of angels, sing in exultation.
   O sing all ye citizens of heaven above.
   Glory to God in the highest.

O Little Town of Bethlehem

Words by Phillips Brooks
Music by Lewis H. Redner

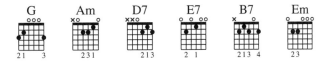

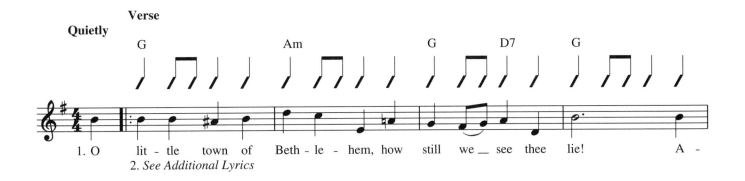

Verse

Quietly

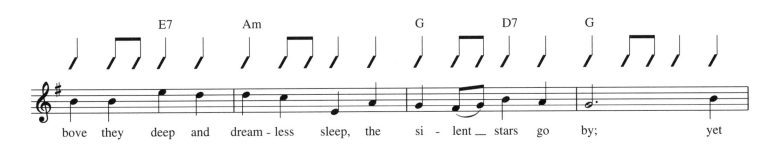

1. O lit-tle town of Beth-le-hem, how still we __ see thee lie! A-
2. *See Additional Lyrics*

bove they deep and dream-less sleep, the si - lent __ stars go by; yet

in thy dark streets shin - eth the ev - er - last - ing light; the

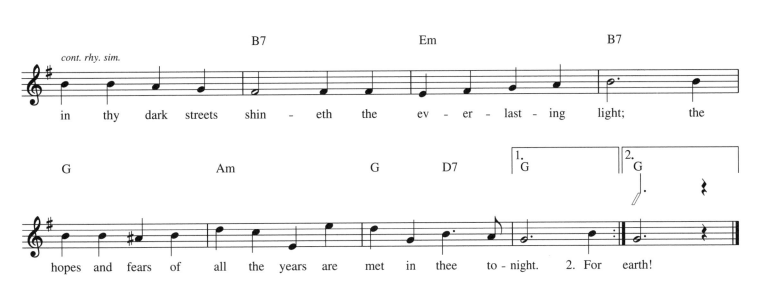

hopes and fears of all the years are met in thee to - night. 2. For earth!

Additional Lyrics

2. For Christ is born of Mary, and gathered all above.
   While mortals sleep the angels keep
   Their watch of wond'ring love.
   O morning stars, together proclaim the holy birth!
   And praises sing to God the King,
   And peace to men on earth!

O Holy Night

English Words by John S. Dwight
Music by Adolphe Adam

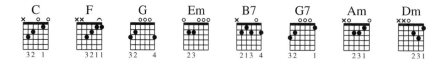

Verse
Slowly

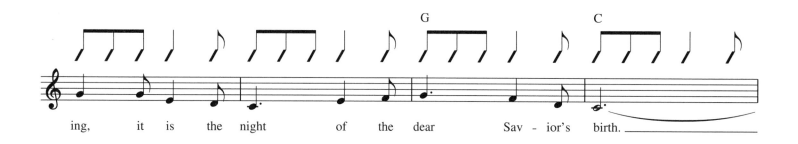

1. O ho - ly night _____ the stars are bright - ly shin -
2. *See Additional Lyrics*

ing, it is the night of the dear Sav - ior's birth. _____

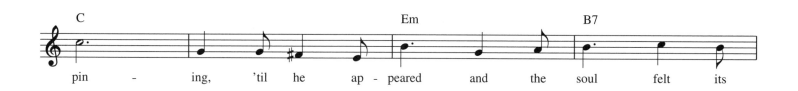

_____ Long lay the world _____ in sin and er - ror

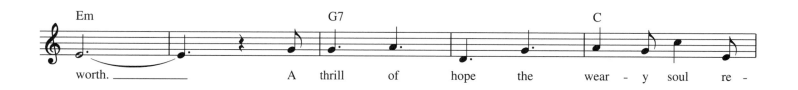

pin - ing, 'til he ap - peared and the soul felt its

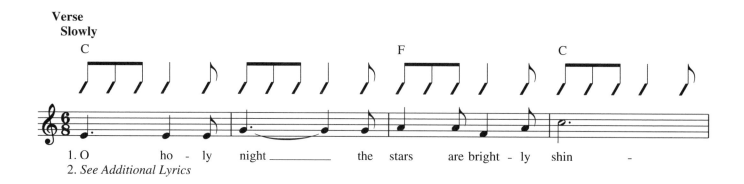

worth. _____ A thrill of hope the wear - y soul re -

joic - es, for yon - der breaks a new and glor - ious morn.

Chorus

Fall _____ on your knees, _____ oh, hear _____ the an - gel
See Additional Lyrics

voic - es! O night _____ di - vine, _____ O

night _____ when Christ was born! _____ O night! _____ O

ho - ly night! O night di - vine! _____

pow'r _____ and glo - ry _____

ev - er - more pro - claim! _____

Additional Lyrics

2. Truly He taught us to love one another.
His law is love, and His gospel is peace.
Chains shall He break, for the slave is our brother,
And in His name all opression shall cease.
Sweet hymns of joy in grateful chorus raise we.
Let all within us praise His holy name.

Chorus Christ is the Lord, oh, praise His name forever!
His pow'r and glory evermore proclaim!
His pow'r and glory evermore proclaim!

Old Toy Trains

Words and Music by Roger Miller

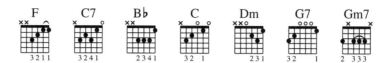

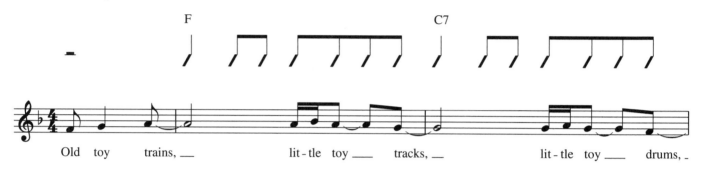

Chorus
Moderately

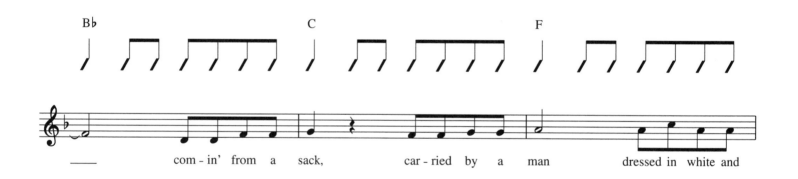

Old toy trains, ___ lit-tle toy ___ tracks, ___ lit-tle toy ___ drums, ___

___ com-in' from a sack, car-ried by a man dressed in white and

red. Lit-tle boy ___ don't ___ you think it's time you were in bed? Close your

Bridge

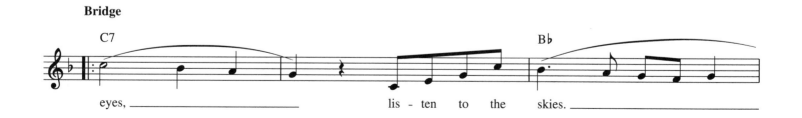

eyes, _____ lis-ten to the skies. _____

All is calm, all is well; soon you'll hear Kris

Chorus

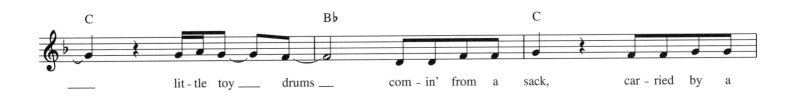

Krin-gle and the jin-gle ___ bell bring-in' lit-tle toy ___ trains, ___ lit-tle toy ___ tracks, ___

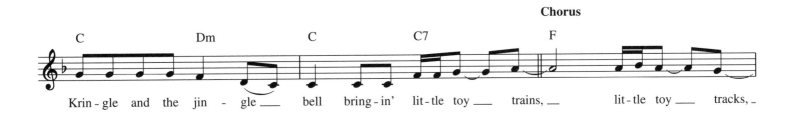

___ lit-tle toy ___ drums ___ com-in' from a sack, car-ried by a

man dressed in white and red. Lit-tle boy ___ don't ___ you think it's time you were in

1.   2.

bed? So close your bed? Lit-tle boy ___ don't ___

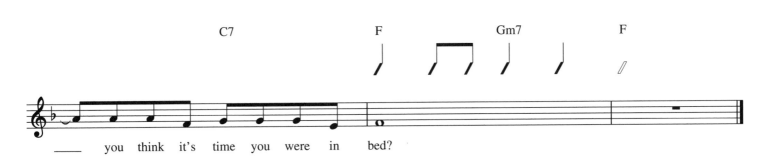

___ you think it's time you were in bed?

One Bright Star

Words and Music by John Jarvis

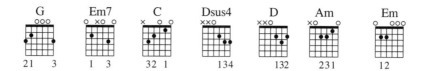

Intro
Moderately slow

Long, long, a - go in a world dark and

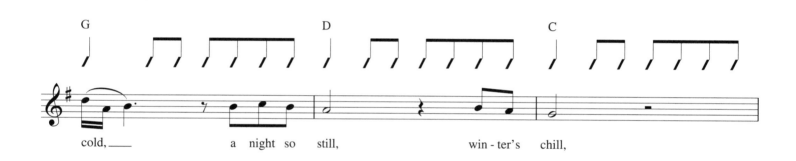

cold, a night so still, win - ter's chill,

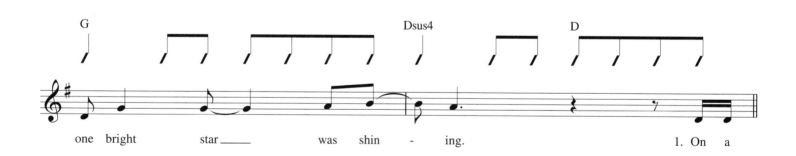

one bright star was shin - ing. 1. On a

Verse

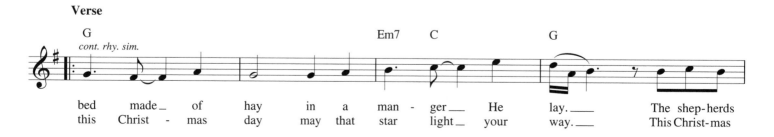

bed made of hay in a man - ger He lay. The shep - herds
this Christ - mas day may that star light your way. This Christ - mas

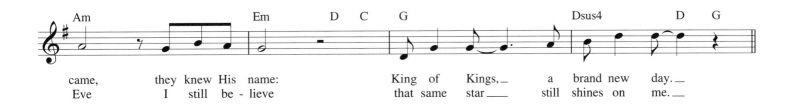

came, they knew His name: King of Kings,— a brand new day.—
Eve I still be - lieve that same star— still shines on me.—

Chorus

They} saw the light— in the dark - ness.— It shines on love— and
I }

ten - der - ness,— brings out the hope— that's in all— of us.— May it

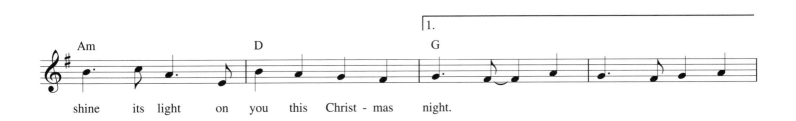

shine its light on you this Christ - mas night.

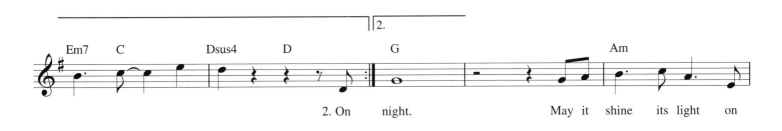

2. On night. May it shine its light on

Outro

you this Christ - mas night.

Rockin' Around the Christmas Tree

Music and Lyrics by Johnny Marks

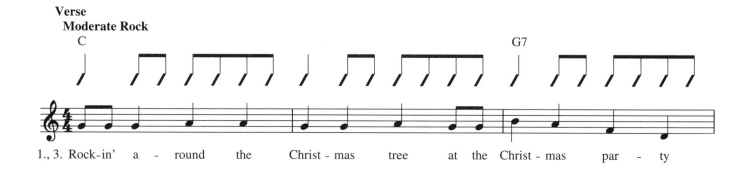

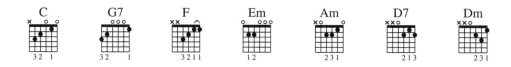

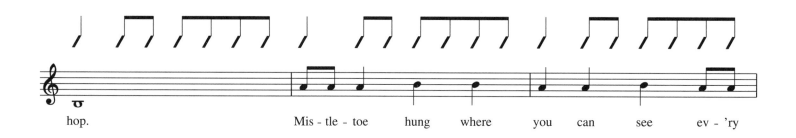

1., 3. Rock-in' a - round the Christ - mas tree at the Christ - mas par - ty

hop. Mis - tle - toe hung where you can see ev - 'ry

cont. rhy. sim.

cou - ple tries to stop. Rock - in' a - round the

Christ - mas tree, let the Christ - mas spir - it ring. La - ter we'll have some

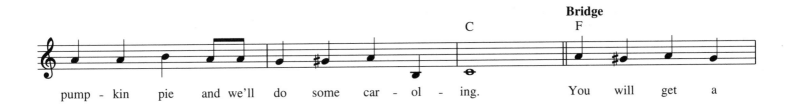

pump - kin   pie   and we'll   do   some   car - ol - ing.   You   will   get   a

sen - ti - men - tal   feel - ing   when   you   hear   voic - es   sing - ing,

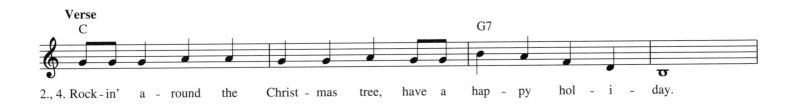

"Let's   be   jol - ly.   Deck   the   halls   with   boughs   of   hol - ly."

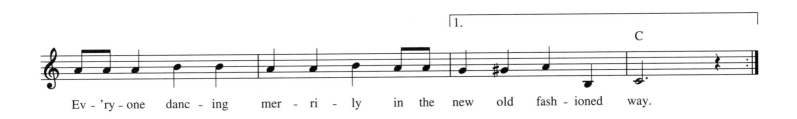

2., 4. Rock - in'   a - round   the   Christ - mas   tree,   have   a   hap - py   hol - i - day.

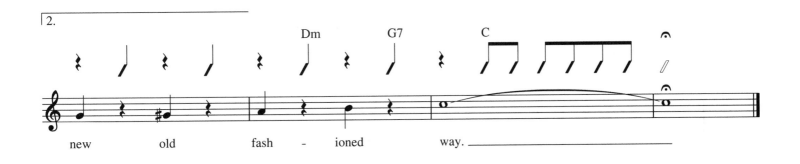

Ev - 'ry - one   danc - ing   mer - ri - ly   in   the   new   old   fash - ioned   way.

new   old   fash - ioned   way. _____

Rudolph the Red-Nosed Reindeer

Music and Lyrics by Johnny Marks

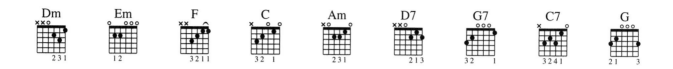

Intro
Rubato

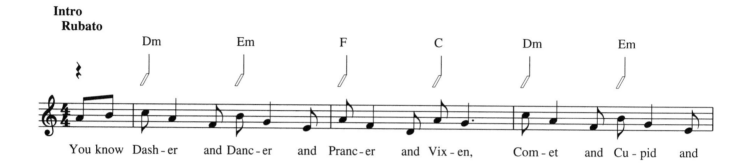

You know Dash-er and Danc-er and Pranc-er and Vix-en, Com-et and Cu-pid and

Don-ner and Blitz-en, but do you re-call the most fa-mous rein-deer of all?

Verse
Lightly

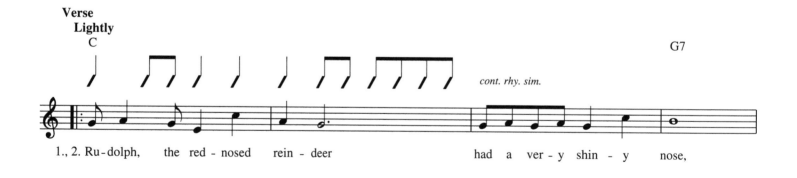

1., 2. Ru-dolph, the red-nosed rein-deer had a ver-y shin-y nose,

and if you ev-er saw it, you would e-ven say it glows.

All of the oth - er rein - deer used to laugh and call him names,

they nev - er let poor Ru - dolph join in an - y rein - deer games.

Bridge

Then one fog - gy Christ - mas Eve, San - ta came to say,

"Ru - dolph, with your nose so bright, won't you guide my sleigh to - night?"

Outro

Then how the rein - deer loved him as they shout - ed out with glee;

1.

"Ru - dolph, the red - nosed rein - deer, you'll go down in his - to - ry!"

2.

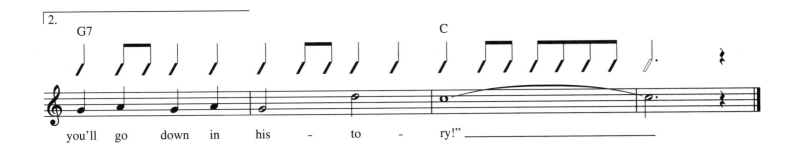

you'll go down in his - to - ry!"

Santa Baby

By Joan Javits, Phil Springer and Tony Springer

_____ Santa ba - by, so hur - ry down the chim - ney to - night. _____

Bridge

Think of all the fun I've missed. _ Think of all the fel - las that I
See Additional Lyrics

have - n't kissed. _ Next year I could be just as good _ if you check off my

Verse

Christ - mas list. 3. San - ta ba - by, I want a yacht and real - ly that's not ___ a lot; ___
6. *See Additional Lyrics*

been an an - gel all year. ___ San - ta ba - by, so hur - ry down the chim - ney to - night. _

Additional Lyrics

4. Santa baby, one little thing I really do need;
The deed to a platinum mine.
Santa honey, so hurry down the chimney tonight.

5. Santa cutie and fill my stocking with a duplex and cheques.
Sign your X on the line.
Santa cutie, and hurry down the chimney tonight.

Bridge Come and trim my Christmas tree
With some decorations at Tiffany.
I really do believe in you.
Let's see if you believe in me.

6. Santa baby, forgot to mention one little thing, a ring!
I don't mean on the phone.
Santa baby, so hurry down the chimney tonight.

Silent Night

Words by Joseph Mohr
Translated by John F. Young
Music by Franz X. Gruber

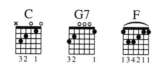

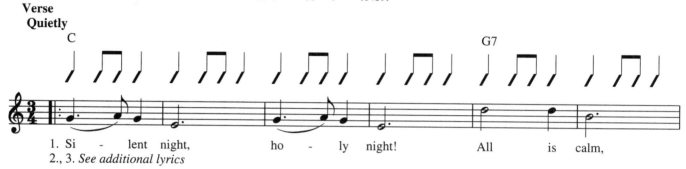

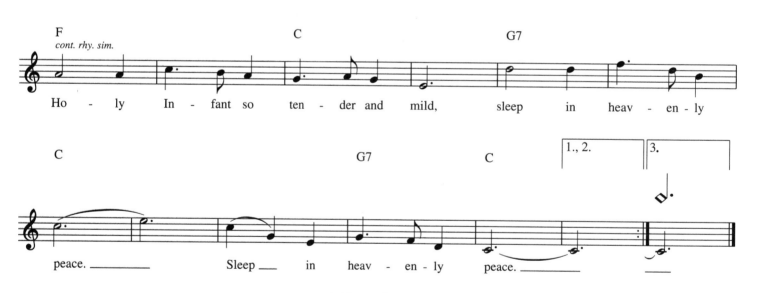

Additional Lyrics

2. Silent night, holy night!
   Shepherds quake at the sight.
   Glories stream from heaven afar.
   Heavenly hosts sing Alleluia.
   Christ the Savior is born!
   Christ the Savior is born!

3. Silent night, holy night!
   Son of God, love's pure light.
   Radiant beams from thy holy face
   With the dawn of redeeming grace.
   Jesus Lord at Thy birth.
   Jesus Lord at Thy birth.

Silver and Gold

Music and Lyrics by Johnny Marks

Silver Bells

from the Paramount Picture THE LEMON DROP KID

Words and Music by Jay Livingston and Ray Evans

Additional Lyrics

2. Strings of street lights even stop lights
   Blink a bright red and green,
   As the shoppers rush home with their treasures.
   Hear the snow crunch, see the kids bunch,
   This is Santa's big scene,
   And above all the bustle you hear:

Snowfall

Lyrics by Ruth Thornhill
Music by Claude Thornhill

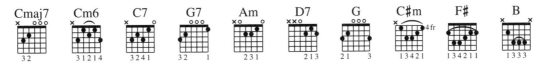

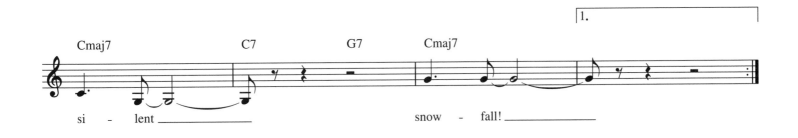

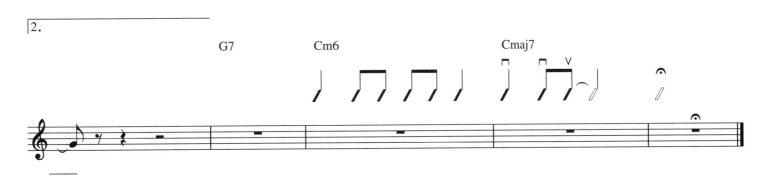

Suzy Snowflake

Words and Music by Sid Tepper and Roy Bennett

Up on the Housetop

Words and Music by B.R. Handy

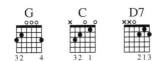

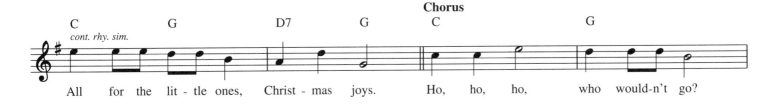

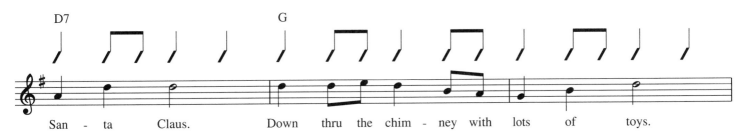

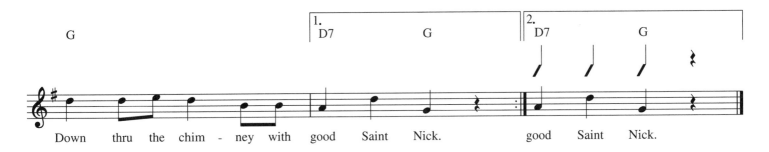

Additional Lyrics

2. First comes the stocking of Little Nell,
   Oh, dear Santa, fill it well.
   Give her a dollie that laughs and cries,
   One that will open and shut her eyes.

This Is Christmas
(Bright, Bright the Holly Berries)

Lyric by Wihla Hutson
Music by Alfred Burt

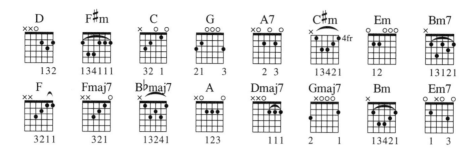

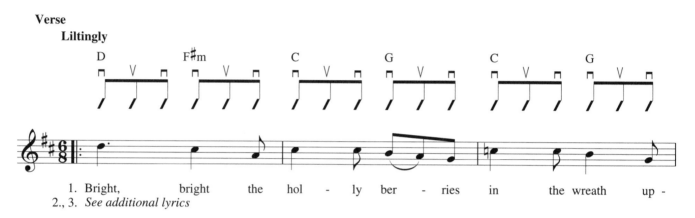

Verse
Liltingly

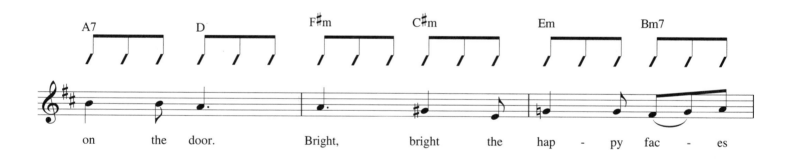

1. Bright,   bright the hol - ly ber - ries in the wreath up-
2., 3. *See additional lyrics*

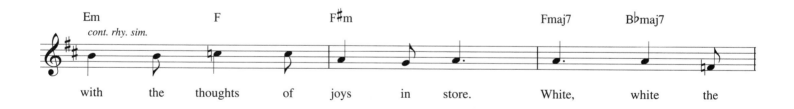

on the door.   Bright,   bright the hap - py fac - es

with the thoughts of joys in store.   White,   white the

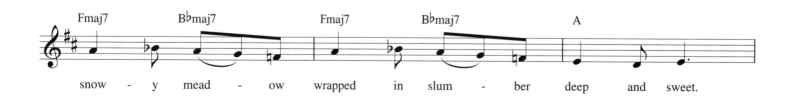

snow - y mead - ow wrapped in slum - ber deep and sweet.

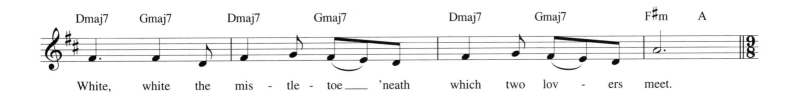

White, white the mis - tle - toe ____ 'neath which two lov - ers meet.

Chorus

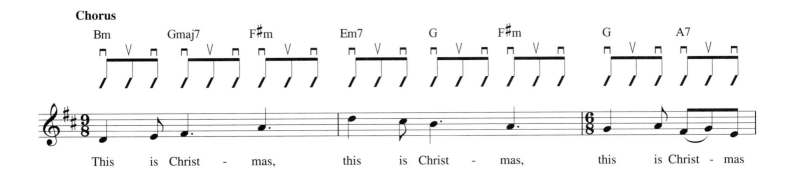

This is Christ - mas, this is Christ - mas, this is Christ - mas

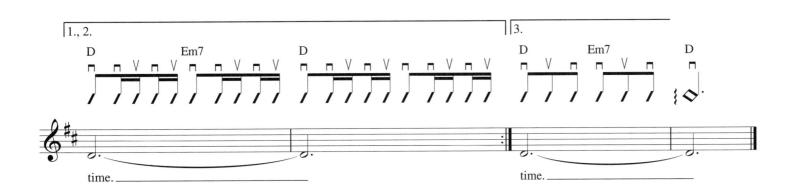

1., 2. time. ____

3. time. ____

Additional Lyrics

2. Gay, gay the children's voices filled with laughter, filled with glee.
Gay, gay the tinsled things upon the dark and spicy tree.
Day, day when all mankind may hear the angel's song again.
Day, day when Christ was born to bless the sons of men.

3. Sing, sing ye heav'nly host to tell the blessed Saviour's birth.
Sing, sing in holy joy, ye dwellers all upon the earth.
King, King yet tiny Babe, come down to us from God above.
King, King of ev'ry heart which opens wide to love.

'Twas the Night Before Christmas

Words by Clement Clark Moore
Music by F. Henri Klickman

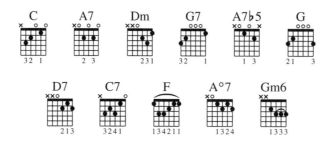

Brightly   **Verse**

1. 'Twas the   night be - fore   Christ - mas, when   all   through the house,   not   a   crea-ture was   stir - ring, not
2. - 7. See Additional Lyrics

e - ven   a mouse. The   stock-ings were   hung   by   the   chim - ney with   care,   in

cont. rhy. sim.

hopes   that Saint Nich - o - las   soon   would be   there.   The   chil - dren were   nest - led   all

snug   in   their beds,   while   vis - ions   of   su - gar plums   danced through their heads.   And

Ma - ma in her 'ker - chief and I in my cap, had just

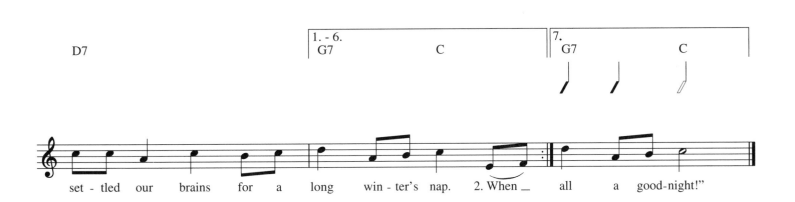

set - tled our brains for a long win - ter's nap. 2. When ___ all a good-night!"

Additional Lyrics

2. When out on the lawn there arouse such a clatter;
   I sprang from my bed to see what was the matter.
   Away to the window I flew like a flash,
   Tore open the shutters and threw up the sash.
   The moon, on the breast of the new-fallen snow,
   Gave a lustre of midday to objects below.
   When what to my wondering eyes should appear.
   But a miniature sleigh and eight tiny reindeer.

3. With a little old driver; so lively and quick,
   I knew in a moment it must be Saint Nick.
   More rapid than eagles, his coursers they came
   And he whistled, and shouted, and called them by name;
   "Now, Dasher, Now, Dancer! Now, Prancer! Now, Vixen!
   On Comet! On, Cupid! On Donder and Blitzen!
   To the top of the porch, to the top of the wall!
   Now dash away, dash away, dash away all!"

4. As dry leaves that before the wild hurricane fly,
   When they meet with an obstacle, mount to the sky.
   So up to the house-top the coursers they flew,
   With the sleigh full of toys, and Saint Nicholas, too.
   And then in a twinkling I heard on the roof
   The prancing and pawing of each little hoof.
   As I drew in my head, and was turning around,
   Down the chimney Saint Nicholas came with a bound.

5. He was dressed all in fir from his head to his foot
   And his clothes were all tarnished with ashes and soot.
   And he looked like a peddler just opening his pack.
   His eyes how they twinkled! His dimples how merry!
   His cheeks were like roses, his nose like a cherry,
   His droll little mouth was drawn up like a bow
   And the beard of his chin was as white as the snow.

6. The stump of a pipe he held tight in his teeth
   And the smoke, it encircled his head like a wreath.
   He had a broad face, and a round little belly
   That shook, when he laughed, like a bowl full of jelly.
   He was chubby and plump, a right jolly old elf,
   And I laughed when I saw him, in spite of myself.
   A wink of his eye and a twist of his head,
   Soon gave me to know I had nothing to dread.

7. He spoke not a word but went straight to his work,
   And filled all the stockings, then turned with a jerk,
   And laying his finger aside of his nose,
   And giving a nod, up the chimney he rose.
   He sprang to his sleigh, to his team gave a whistle
   And away they all flew like the down of a thistle,
   But I heard him exclaim, ere he drove out of sight:
   "Happy Christmas to all, and all a good-night!"

The Twelve Days of Christmas

Traditional English Carol

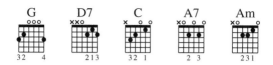

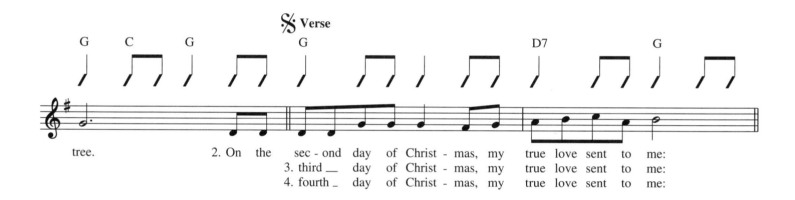

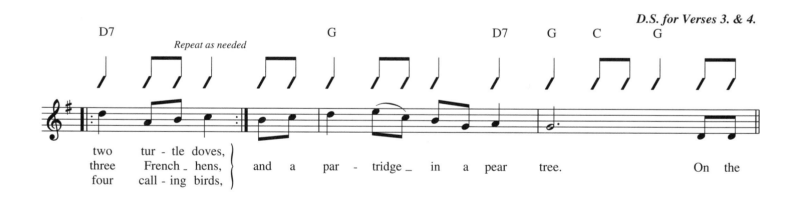

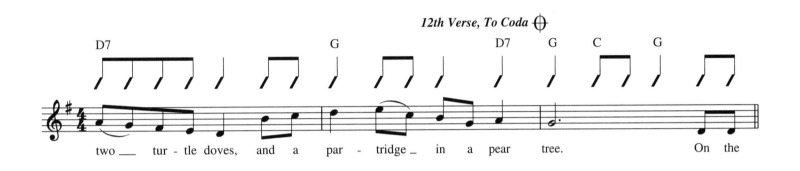

12th Verse, To Coda ⊕

Verse

6. sixth ___ day of Christ - mas, my true love sent to me:
7. sev - enth day of Christ - mas, my true love sent to me:
8. eighth ___ day of Christ - mas, my true love sent to me:
9. ninth ___ day of Christ - mas, my true love sent to me:
10. tenth ___ day of Christ - mas, my true love sent to me:
11. 'lev - enth day of Christ - mas, my true love sent to me:
12. twelfth ___ day of Christ - mas, my true love sent to me:

⊕ Coda

D.S.S. for Verses 7. - 12.

Repeat as needed

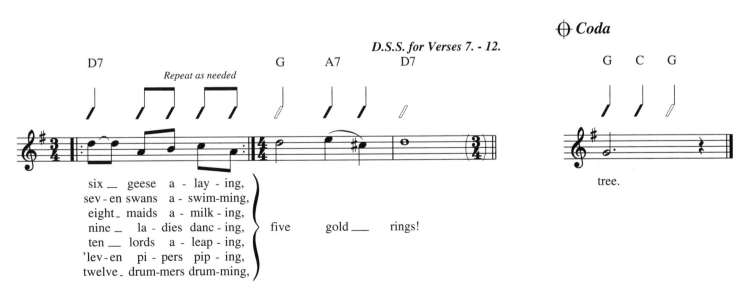

six ___ geese a - lay - ing,
sev - en swans a - swim - ming,
eight ___ maids a - milk - ing,
nine ___ la - dies danc - ing,   five gold ___ rings!
ten ___ lords a - leap - ing,
'lev - en pi - pers pip - ing,
twelve ___ drum - mers drum - ming,

tree.

We Need a Little Christmas

from MAME

Music and Lyric by Jerry Herman

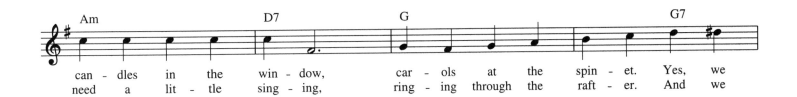

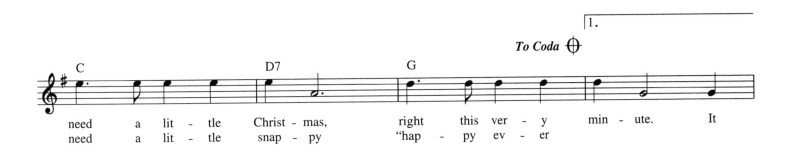

can - dles in the win - dow, car - ols at the spin - et. Yes, we
need a lit - tle sing - ing, ring - ing through the raft - er. And we

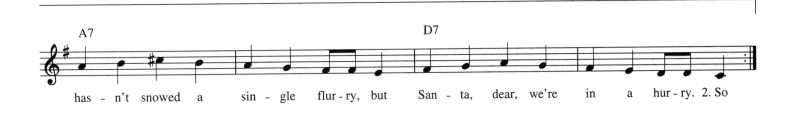

To Coda

need a lit - tle Christ - mas, right this ver - y min - ute. It
need a lit - tle snap - py "hap - py ev - er

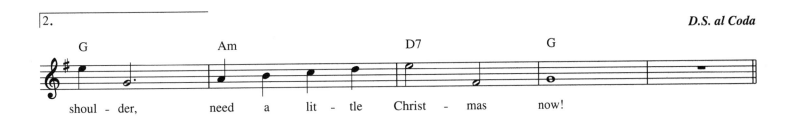

has - n't snowed a sin - gle flur - ry, but San - ta, dear, we're in a hur - ry. 2. So

2. | D.S. al Coda

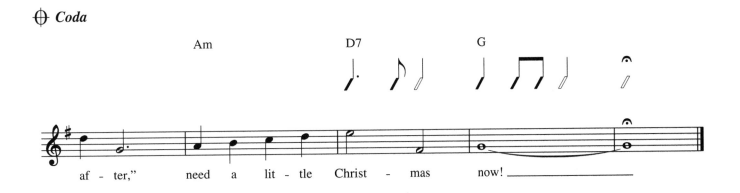

shoul - der, need a lit - tle Christ - mas now!

Coda

af - ter," need a lit - tle Christ - mas now! _____

Additional Lyrics

2. So climb down the chimney,
Turn on the brightest string of lights I've ever seen.
Slice up the fruitcake.
It's time we hung some tinsel on the evergreen bough.
For I've grown a little leaner, grown a little colder,
Grown a little sadder, grown a little older,
And I need a little angel, sitting on my shoulder,
Need a little Christmas now!

We Three Kings of Orient Are

Words and Music by John H. Hopkins

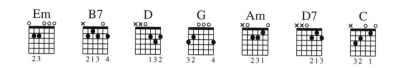

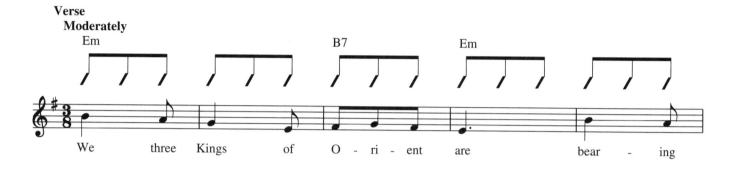

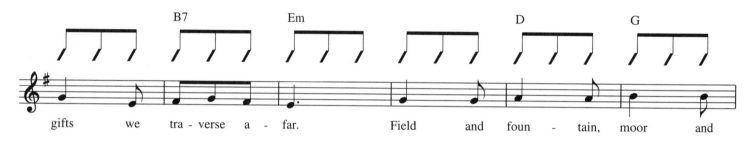

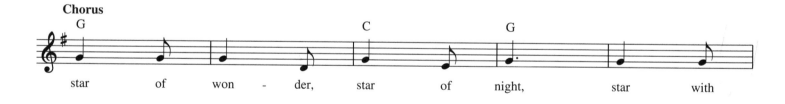

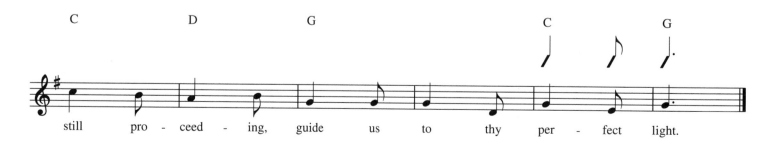

We Wish You a Merry Christmas

Traditional English Folksong

Additional Lyrics

2. We all know that Santa's coming.
We all know that Santa's coming.
We all know that Santa's coming
And soon will be here.

What Are You Doing New Year's Eve?

By Frank Loesser

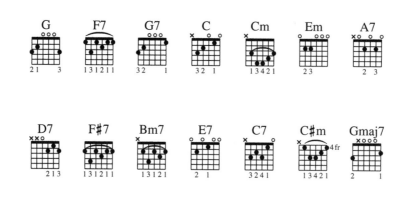

Verse
Moderately

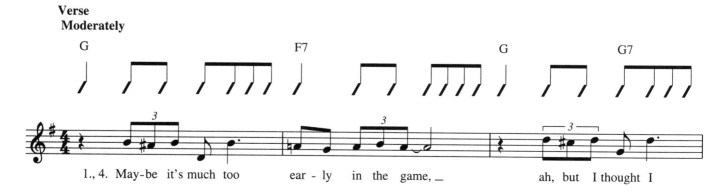

1., 4. May-be it's much too ear-ly in the game, __ ah, but I thought I

ask you just the same, __ what are you do-ing new year's, New Year's

Verse

cont. rhy. sim.

Eve? 2., 5. Won-der whose arms will hold you good and tight, __

when it's ex-act-ly twelve o'-clock that night, __ wel-com-ing in the

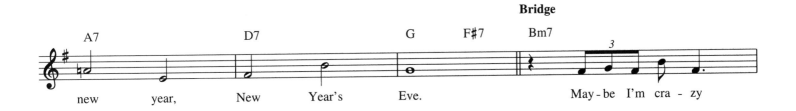

Bridge

A7 ... D7 ... G ... F#7 ... Bm7

new year, New Year's Eve. May-be I'm cra-zy

E7 ... C7 ... Bm7 ... C#m ... C7

to sup - pose I'd ev - er be the one you chose

Bm7 ... Gmaj7 ... E7 ... A7

out of the thou - sand in - vi - ta - tions you'll re -

Verse

D7 ... G ... F7

ceive. 3., 6. Ah, but in case I stand one lit - tle chance, —

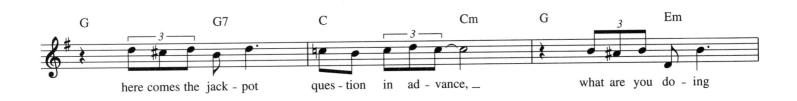

G ... G7 ... C ... Cm ... G ... Em

here comes the jack - pot ques - tion in ad - vance, — what are you do - ing

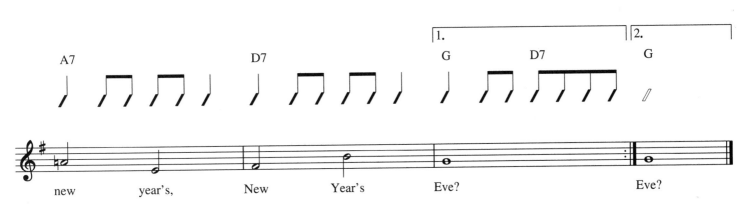

1. ... 2.

A7 ... D7 ... G ... D7 ... G

new year's, New Year's Eve? Eve?

Wonderful Christmastime

Words and Music by McCartney

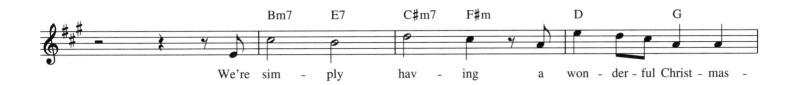

We're sim – ply hav – ing a won – der – ful Christ – mas –

D.C. al Coda
(take 2nd ending)

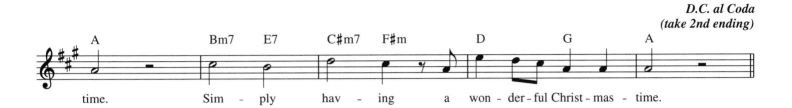

time. Sim – ply hav – ing a won – der – ful Christ – mas – time.

⊕ *Coda*

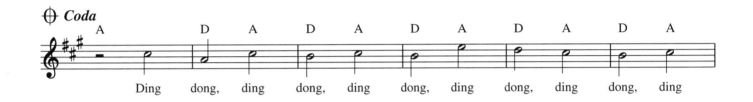

Ding dong, ding dong, ding dong, ding dong, ding dong, ding

dong, dong dong, dong, dong. The par – ty's on, ____ the spir – it's up, _

____ we're here to – night _ and that's e – nough. _

Outro-Chorus

Repeat & Fade

Sim – ply hav – ing a won – der – ful Christ – mas – time. We're

Additional Lyrics

2. The party's on,
   The feeling's here
   That only comes
   This time of year.

3. The word is out
   About the town,
   To lift a glass.
   Oh, don't look down.

You Make It Feel Like Christmas

Words and Music by Neil Diamond

You're Not Alone

Words and Music by Shawn Stockman

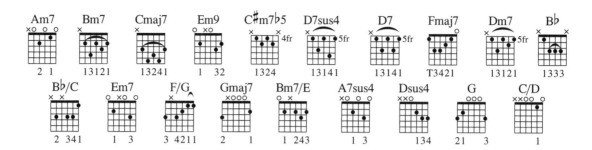

Tune down ½ step:
(low to high) E♭ - A♭ - D♭ - G♭ - B♭ - E♭

Intro
Moderately slow

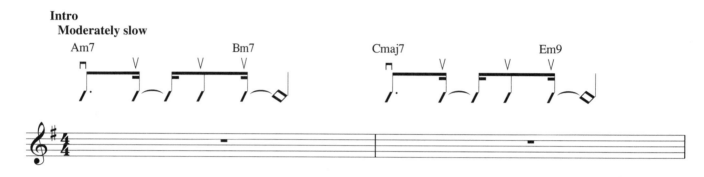

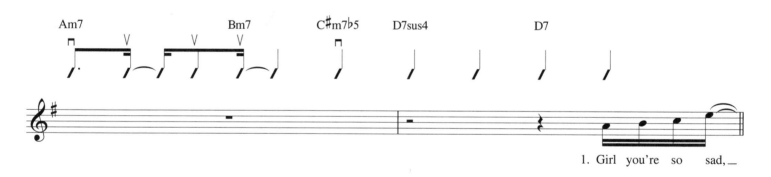

1. Girl you're so sad, ___

Verse

___ he was the ver-y first love___ you had ___ but he hurt___ your heart___ real bad.___
2., 3., 4. *See additional lyrics*

___ He just led___ your feel-ings a-stray, ___ and on a hol-i-day. Go 'head and cry,___

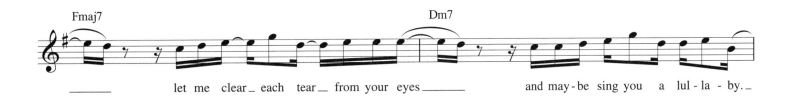

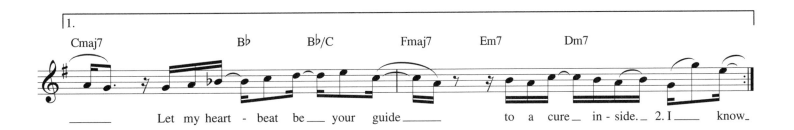

let me clear_ each tear_ from your eyes _____ and may-be sing you a lul-la-by._

1.
Let my heart - beat be_ your guide _____ to a cure_ in - side._ 2. I ___ know_

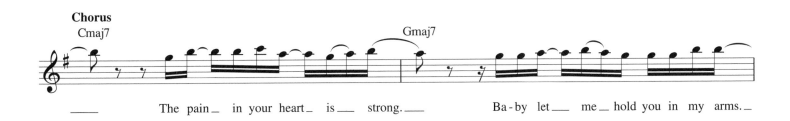

2.
gain. I ___ can be_ the_ key_ for your heart_ to mend. 'Cause ba - by you're not a - lone.___

Chorus
The pain_ in your heart_ is_ strong.___ Ba - by let ___ me_ hold you in my arms.___

Let me be ___ your pro-tec - tor from harm.___ 'Cause no ___ one should be ___ a - lone

To Coda
on Christ - mas._____

D.S. al Coda
(take repeat)   **Coda**

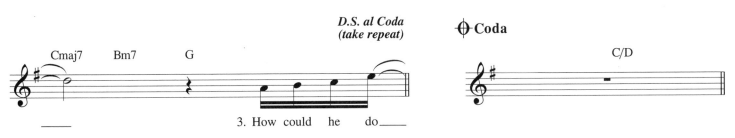

3. How could he do___

Interlude

Spoken: Girl, this Christmas you won't be alone, you don't have to cry, you don't have to worry about a thing.
Don't live in the past, baby, I'm your future. All the feelings that I have are for you. And anything that I can do to take away any problem that you

1.

All the gifts that you wanted this year are yours. You dont have to worry 'bout him no more 'cause he's gone.

2.

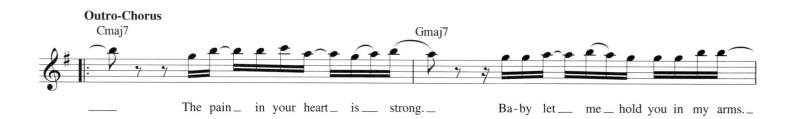

may have or have had, I'm here. Just say, "Michael" and this Christmas is yours.   'Cause ba - by you're not   a - lone.

Outro-Chorus

_____   The pain _ in your heart _ is _ strong. _   Ba-by let _ me _ hold you in my arms. _

Repeat and fade

_____   Let me be _ your pro - tec - tor from harm, _   'cause no _ one should be _____ a- lone. _

Additional Lyrics

2. I know that it's, oh, so hard to let go.
   Give yourself time to heal, take it, slow.
   Let's talk as the rainbow colored lights make the tree glow.
   I'm your friend, I will be here for you 'til the end
   'Cause I don't wanna see you hurt again.
   I can be the key for your heart to mend.

3. How could he do such a thing to one as good as you?
   Gave him your all and I know that it's true.
   Had a gem and didn't know what to do.
   But baby I'm here to tell you that I'm yours if you want me.
   These feelings I've held in too long. You've been on my mind.
   Girl, you know I'll never find love that's so kind.

4. I open up to pray that by the Lord's grace you would come my
   Way and receive love that won't go away.
   Celebrate this occasion with gifts of joy on His birthday.
   On this night, I'll fill all your empty spaces inside.
   Hold you close and make ev'rything alright,
   'Cause this day is for sharing and no one should be without someone caring.

· AUTHENTIC CHORDS · ORIGINAL KEYS · COMPLETE SONGS ·

The *Strum It* series lets players strum the chords and sing along with their favorite hits. Each song has been selected because it can be played with regular open chords, barre chords, or other moveable chord types. Guitarists can simply play the rhythm, or play and sing along through the entire song. All songs are shown in their original keys complete with chords, strum patterns, melody and lyrics. Wherever possible, the chord voicings from the recorded versions are notated.

Acoustic Classics

Play along with the recordings of 21 acoustic classics. Songs include: And I Love Her • Angie • Barely Breathing • Free Fallin' • Maggie May • Melissa • Mr. Jones • Only Wanna Be with You • Patience • Signs • Teach Your Children • Wonderful Tonight • Wonderwall • Yesterday • and more.
00699238 $10.95

The Beatles Favorites

Features 23 classic Beatles hits, including: Can't Buy Me Love • Eight Days a Week • Hey Jude • I Saw Her Standing There • Let It Be • Nowhere Man • She Loves You • Something • Yesterday • You've Got to Hide Your Love Away • and more.
00699249 $14.95

Celtic Guitar Songbook

Features 35 complete songs in their original keys, with authentic chords, strum patterns, melody and lyrics. Includes: Black Velvet Band • Cockles and Mussels (Molly Malone) • Danny Boy (Londonderry Air) • Finnegan's Wake • Galway Bay • I'm a Rover and Seldom Sober • The Irish Washerwoman • Kerry Dance • Killarney • McNamara's Band • My Wild Irish Rose • The Rose of Tralee • Sailor's Hornpipe • Whiskey in the Jar • Wild Rover • and more.
00699265 $9.95

Christmas Songs for Guitar

Over 40 Christmas favorites, including: The Christmas Song (Chestnuts Roasting on an Open Fire) • Feliz Navidad • Frosty the Snow Man • Grandma Got Run Over by a Reindeer • The Greatest Gift of All • I'll Be Home for Christmas • It's Beginning to Look Like Christmas • Rockin' Around the Christmas Tree • Silver Bells • and more. 00699247 $9.95

Christmas Songs with Three Chords

30 all-time favorites: Angels We Have Heard on High • Away in a Manger • Deck the Hall • Go, Tell It on the Mountain • Here We Come A-Wassailing • I Heard the Bells on Christmas Day • Jolly Old St. Nicholas • Silent Night • Up on the Housetop • and more.
00699487 $8.95

Country Strummin'

Features 24 songs: Achy Breaky Heart • Adalida • Ain't That Lonely Yet • Blue • The Beaches of Cheyenne • A Broken Wing • Gone Country • I Fall to Pieces • My Next Broken Heart • She and I • Unchained Melody • What a Crying Shame • and more.
00699119 $8.95

Jim Croce - Classic Hits

Authentic chords to 22 great songs from Jim Croce, including: Bad, Bad Leroy Brown • I'll Have to Say I Love You in a Song • Operator (That's Not the Way It Feels) • Time in a Bottle • and more.
00699269 $10.95

Disney Favorites

A great collection of 34 easy-to-play Disney favorites. Includes: Can You Feel the Love Tonight • Circle of Life • Cruella De Vil • Friend Like Me • It's a Small World • Some Day My Prince Will Come • Under the Sea • Whistle While You Work • Winnie the Pooh • Zero to Hero • and more. 00699171 $10.95

Disney Greats

Easy arrangements with guitar chord frames and strum patterns for 39 wonderful Disney classics including: Arabian Nights • The Aristocats • Beauty and the Beast • Colors of the Wind • Go the Distance • Hakuna Matata • Heigh-Ho • Kiss the Girl • A Pirate's Life • When You Wish Upon a Star • Zip-A-Dee-Doo-Dah • Theme from Zorro • and more. 00699172 $10.95

Best of The Doors

Strum along with more than 25 of your favorite hits from The Doors. Includes: Been Down So Long • Hello I Love You Won't You Tell Me Your Name? • Light My Fire • Riders on the Storm • Touch Me • and more. 00699177 $10.95

Favorite Songs with 3 Chords

27 popular songs that are easy to play, including: All Shook Up • Blue Suede Shoes • Boot Scootin' Boogie • Evil Ways • Great Balls of Fire • Lay Down Sally • Semi-Charmed Life • Surfin' U.S.A. • Twist and Shout • Wooly Bully • and more.
00699112 $8.95

Favorite Songs with 4 Chords

22 tunes in this great collection, including: Beast of Burden • Don't Be Cruel • Get Back • Gloria • I Fought the Law • La Bamba • Last Kiss • Let Her Cry • Love Stinks • Peggy Sue • 3 AM • Wild Thing • and more. 00699270 $8.95

Irving Berlin's God Bless America

25 patriotic anthems: Amazing Grace • America, the Beautiful • Battle Hymn of the Republic • From a Distance • God Bless America • Imagine • The Lord's Prayer • The Star Spangled Banner • Stars and Stripes Forever • This Land Is Your Land • United We Stand • You're a Grand Old Flag • and more.
00699508 $9.95

Great '50s Rock

28 of early rock's biggest hits, including: At the Hop • Blueberry Hill • Bye Bye Love • Hound Dog • Rock Around the Clock • That'll Be the Day • and more. 00699187 $8.95

Great '60s Rock

Features the chords, strum patterns, melody and lyrics for 27 classic rock songs, all in their original keys. Includes: And I Love Her • Crying • Gloria • Good Lovin' • I Fought the Law • Mellow Yellow • Return to Sender • Runaway • Surfin' U.S.A. • The Twist • Twist and Shout • Under the Boardwalk • Wild Thing • and more. 00699188 $8.95

Great '70s Rock

Strum the chords to 21 classic '70s hits! Includes: Band on the Run • Burning Love • If • It's a Heartache • Lay Down Sally • Let It Be • Love Hurts • Maggie May • New Kid in Town • Ramblin' Man • Time for Me to Fly • Two Out of Three Ain't Bad • Wild World • and more. 00699262 $8.95

Great '80s Rock

23 arrangements that let you play along with your favorite recordings from the 1980s, such as: Back on the Chain Gang • Centerfold • Crazy Little Thing Called Love • Free Fallin' • Got My Mind Set on You • Kokomo • Should I Stay or Should I Go • Uptown Girl • Waiting for a Girl Like You • What I Like About You • and more. 00699263 $8.95

Best of Woody Guthrie

20 of the Guthrie's most popular songs, including: Do Re Mi • The Grand Coulee Dam • I Ain't Got No Home • Ramblin' Round • Roll On, Columbia • So Long It's Been Good to Know Yuh (Dusty Old Dust) • Talking Dust Bowl • This Land Is Your Land • Tom Joad • and more. 00699496 $12.95

The John Hiatt Collection

This collection includes 17 classics: Angel Eyes • Feels Like Rain • Have a Little Faith in Me • Memphis in the Meantime • Perfectly Good Guitar • A Real Fine Love • Riding with the King • Thing Called Love (Are You Ready for This Thing Called Love) • The Way We Make a Broken Heart • and more.
00699398 $12.95

Hymn Favorites

Includes: Amazing Grace • Battle Hymn of the Republic • Down by the Riverside • Holy, Holy, Holy • Just as I Am • Rock of Ages • This Is My Father's World • What a Friend We Have in Jesus • and more. 00699271 $9.95

Best of Sarah McLachlan

20 of Sarah's most popular hits for guitar, including: Adia • Angel • Building a Mystery • I Will Remember You • Ice Cream • Sweet Surrender • and more. 00699231 $10.95

A Merry Christmas Songbook

Easy arrangements for 51 holiday hits: Away in a Manger • Deck the Hall • Fum, Fum, Fum • The Holly and the Ivy • Jolly Old St. Nicholas • O Christmas Tree • Star of the East • The Twelve Days of Christmas • and more! 00699211 $8.95

Pop-Rock Guitar Favorites

31 songs, including: Angie • Brown Eyed Girl • Crazy Little Thing Called Love • Eight Days a Week • Fire and Rain • Free Bird • Gloria • Hey Jude • Let It Be • Maggie May • New Kid in Town • Surfin' U.S.A. • Wild Thing • Wonderful Tonight • and more. 00699088 $8.95

Best of George Strait

Strum the chords to 20 great Strait hits! Includes: Adalida • All My Ex's Live in Texas • The Best Day • Blue Clear Sky • Carried Away • The Chair • Does Fort Worth Ever Cross Your Mind • Lovebug • Right or Wrong • Write This Down • and more.
00699235 $10.95

Best of Hank Williams Jr.

24 of Hank's signature standards. Includes: Ain't Misbehavin' • All My Rowdy Friends Are Coming Over Tonight • Attitude Adjustment • Family Tradition • Honky Tonkin' • Texas Women • There's a Tear in My Beer • Whiskey Bent and Hell Bound • and more. 00699224 $10.95

Women of Rock

22 hits from today's top female artists. Includes: Bitch • Don't Speak • Galileo • Give Me One Reason • I Don't Want to Wait • Insensitive • Lovefool • Mother Mother • Stay • Torn • You Oughta Know • You Were Meant for Me • Zombie • and more.
00699183 $9.95

Prices, contents & availability subject to change without notice. Disney characters & artwork ©Disney Enterprises, Inc.

0102